SWEET SALES

SUCCESSFUL SALES WITH SYNERGY

DAVID K. SWEET, PH.D.

Cover design by Eileen Rockwell
Interior design by Terry Clifton

For more information on foreign distribution, call 717-530-2122.
Reach us on the Internet: www.soundwisdom.com.

Sound Wisdom
P.O. Box 310
Shippensburg, PA 17257-0310

ISBN 13 TP: 978-0-7684-1133-1
ISBN 13 Ebook: 978-0-7684-1134-8

For Worldwide Distribution, Printed in the U.S.A.
1 2 3 4 5 6 7 8 / 19 18 17 16

"Does a struggling salesman start turning up on a bicycle? No, he turns up in a newer car—perception, yeah? They got to trust me—I'm taking these guys into battle, yeah? And I'm doing my own stapling."

—DAVID BRENT, *The Office*

"A good idea is a good idea forever."

—DAVID BRENT, *The Office*

Adrian: *"Einstein flunked out of school, twice".*

Paulie: *"Is that so"?*

Adrian: *"Yeah. Beethoven was deaf. Helen Keller was blind. I think Rocky's got a good chance".*

—*Rocky*

CONTENTS

FOREWORD

A lot has changed since SweetSales was first released in 2007. We have gone through a global recession, companies have restructured and cut costs in a way that we haven't seen since the Great Depression and companies are in survival mode. Spending in some industries totally disappeared and if you were in sales and lacked the skills to close a deal, then you disappeared the way of the dinosaur.

I watched many companies slip away. Actually, it was more terrible and painful than I feared. They scrambled to cut costs, sacked non-performers with a vengeance, took out loans, scratched and clawed like men being attacked by zombies. Then, the aftermath. It reminded me of some Russian story where there is an old farmer in a barren, snow-covered field shoveling frozen earth trying to dig out a half-rotten, brown turnip. He holds it in the palms of his hands wanders into the house and makes the soup for a shivering family. Over the last few years, salespeople were searching for that rotting turnip just to win a bit of commission to feed their own families.

On the other hand, many sales professionals survived and some even thrived. They were diligent, smart, worked harder and longer than everyone else. They targeted the companies making money where there *were* still sales opportunities. As Jeffrey Fox says, "they fished where the fish were". It's good to remember that even in a recession, someone is making money and certain salespeople went into work with this philosophy and pounded the phone, doubled the number of RFPs they delivered and stayed as cool and calm as they could, while others dropped-out around them. Depending on the industry they were in they may not have flourished with the fantastic commissions they had before, but they made sales, kept the company afloat and made it through the hard times.

Through this time many of my own ideas were challenged about sales, for me and the teams I coached. Negotiations became tougher, prospects rarer and sales volumes fewer. Like any animal in a drought, the sales animal used what worked. Fancy sales systems and processes that slick trainers had handed out either worked or they didn't. If they did, they were used, if not, they were trashed. In fact some of my thoughts of what made a good salesperson shifted, while other beliefs were confirmed.

On the whole, "sales systems" tended to fail. In contrast, companies that had solid processes that were followed tended to flourish. Processes were documented, refined, practiced and refined some more. Those that tried to wing-it in a meeting with a business owner or procurement person were more often than not shown the door! Whereas those who succeeded still planned and also tried to understand the customer's needs. Those who forgot how to prospect, died a quick death. Those who worked extra hours and pushed a bit harder to find and close a prospect, survived. Those who were satisfied with their skills and felt sure about what they knew, they found the ground evaporate below their feet. By contrast those who continued to read, studied their products or services, learn soft-skills, conducted role-plays and built upon their knowledge – they survived and sometimes even flourished.

This led me to go back and look at my own sales, to review what I had written and taught salespeople in the U.S. and Asia and then assess how it held up over time. To my surprise I found the principles outlined in most of the pages still held true. The main reason I believe is that I refrain from having a system. Each company is different, every sales person has strengths and weaknesses. There isn't one medicine that cures every ailing patient. In sales, like life, there are no "rules" that need to be followed, or magical step-by-step ways to work a funnel and close a deal, or "musts" that come from empirical research. I believe a more organic approach as used by a farmer: plant, nurture, reap. There are no shortcuts. Mine, is the "keep the pragmatic and rid myself of the rest" sort of philosophy. Sure, I borrow like crazy from solid and practiced systems, but I never feel that one system fits all situations. These are tools in my toolbox. Also, many of the ideas are communication skills and the best practices used in sales situations.

At the core I believe that sales and good communications can be reduced to this: (1) Ask good questions (2) Listen (3) Ask follow-up questions and probe deeper for understanding (4) empathize and in that magic sales moment (5) solve a problem and make a sale through your product or service.

Over the years I've interviewed countless people for my teams. I ask them, what makes a good salesperson? Undoubtedly, they answer, "Good communication skills."

"Okay," I reply, "communication is a wide field. What exactly do you mean?"

I guide them to narrow in on their definition and in the end they reply that good communication is what I mentioned above: questions, listening, follow-up questions, empathy and problem solving.

Then I use the now old, worn trick of asking them to sell me a pen, any pen that they want. The conversation usually goes like this:

> Interviewee: Um, Hi, I would like to sell you this pen.
>
> Me: Great.
>
> Interviewee: This is a super pen! It comes in different colors and writes so smoothly, try it out. It matches your eyes and makes your suit look great.
>
> Me: Thanks, but I use pencils.
>
> Interviewee: Oh.

I point out that they have just told me what makes a good salesperson, they defined it in great communication and knew all the parts. But when it came to the actual implementation, they fall back on the clichéd ideas that a salesperson talks and talks and talks.

Every once in awhile, maybe 1 out of 50 people, will ask questions.

> Interviewee: Thank you for taking time out to see me. Do you use pens?
>
> Me: Yes. (Always learn from your mistakes!)
>
> Interviewee: Great! What kind of pens do you use?
>
> Me: Well, Bic, usually. Just plain pens. I'm always losing them.

Interviewee: What do you like about your pens?

Me: I like them because they're inexpensive and if I lose them, I don't really care.

Interviewee: I know what you mean. What's your preference for colors? (Nice open ended question.)

Me: I use purple pens at home to write in my journal!

Interviewee: Purple? What a great color! What other colors? (Positive response, followed by a follow-up question. Never just accept the first answer given!)

Me: I use green to correct my writing and red for notes and black for formal. I'm kind of selective and really like specific colors for specific times.

Interviewee: Great reason. I love it! What do you dislike about your pens?

Me: Because I love different colors, I always need to buy my pens separately. I would really love to buy them all together.

You can see the difference. The interviewee takes their time and communicates. She asks questions, listens to the answer, asks follow-up questions, empathizes and then when she knows the issues at hand, finally starts to work together with the customer to solve the problem. Clear as vodka.

Not quite. Over the years, I've also noticed another element, one which I've tried to capture in this edition of SweetSales. It's an intangible quality rarely shared with others except after a couple of glasses of Merlot and a philosophical conversation late at night. All Sales Directors know the quality. They can smell it. It's a quality that is in the person's DNA, their being. It's a quality that has the person hard-wired into selling. There is a mindset that is needed for success, a competitive edge.

Another skill Sales Directors would rather neglect is luck. General Napoleon, when interviewing officers for leadership roles, would ask one question: "How lucky are you?" I still find this a relevant question to ask salespeople. I also believe that you create your own luck. If you look at some of the Nobel Prizes in science, for example, you will find that the break-through discoveries were based on luck. But notice that the luck was in the scientist's field of expertise, not in a random area of life. If you sell real estate, your chances of getting lucky selling a computer system are very remote, though you can do a great many things to increase your luck in selling real estate.

Another part that I still maintain in sales is the idea of synergy. I first came into contact with it in my graduate studies when I fell into the writings of R. Buckminster Fuller. The word "synergy" comes from the Greek of "syn-" meaning to combine, where we derive words such as synthesis and synthetic and "ergos" meaning energy or work. To me, the term means to combine in such a way where the whole is greater than the constituent parts. This is fairly consistent with Fuller's idea. I tend to shy away from the more management and corporate ideas of synergy, though the word has gained popularity over the last decade.

Synergy, I believe, is something that a person can make and it will improve a person's life. I believe that great sales, great sales people, the ones with that "plus alpha" factor, are the ones that create the most synergy. They combine their energy and the people around them in such a way that their value is increased. This book will go through the elements that these people, who create synergy around their sales, bring to their sales activity and in doing so make them a success.

Because this book is based on elements, rather than a system, it tends to remain pertinent throughout time. Of course, sales-people need to have in-depth knowledge about their product and/or service, plus time management, territory management and the like and all that is covered here, but communication is at the heart of any sale.

Also, as this book focuses on elements, the information here works for B2B and B2C sales, a service sale and a product sale, a simple sale and a complex sale, consulting and account managing, selling direct, partner sales and retail sales.

This book is also short. Not much theory hides within the pages. Sales people like straight-forward, easy-to-implement ideas. Generally, a sales person does not want *War and Peace* when going through sales guidance. I label most salespeople, myself included, as ADHD. Reading long books with dry passages of theory, scholarly research, facts, figures and tables tends to bore us. You'll not find those here. This is a quick read and some may criticize me for it, but I'd rather leave it simple and easy to read. What I have here is what works. My proof is in the sales, not in class-room studies.

Thank you for going down this path with me. This book is just words from my mind and printed pages. They don't become a reality until they reach your mind and you take action. I hope that you find inspiration and new ideas here that you can put into action. Happy sales to you all! I hope this best of all professions brings you much joy, happiness and prosperity.

DAVID SWEET
Tokyo

INTRODUCTION

Many have said it and I think it is a good thing to remind ourselves that in all actuality, sales is the oldest of all professions. As we explore this profession, we will go through the mental and physical portions of sales, the psychology and communication, as well as some of the tricks of learning how to sell better.

First, we will explore your mindset and how you go into a sales job. If you haven't the right mindset from the start, the rest of what you do will fail. After looking at 14 elements that make up a winning mindset, you'll be asked to rate and work on your own thoughts.

Next, we will investigate what I call "invisible selling" or communication skills. Whenever I speak to sales people, they tell me that communication is the most important skill that they can learn. The reason it is invisible is that it is neither your product nor your service, but the part you bring to the process that can win or hinder the customer from purchasing what you have to sell. You will learn all aspects of communication, verbal and nonverbal communication, spoken and written communication and how each affects your sales.

First, we will consider how you dress, how you act and how the customer experiences you. To better understand how we persuade, we'll explore Aristotle's ideas on persuasion that still guides sales and marketing across the planet.

Next, we will learn to listen—the most important skill in communication.

And then we will explore the fascinating world of nonverbal communication and how we can use our bodies to mirror our sales message. We think that sales people are fast talkers. In truth, sales people are the best questioners: they ask deep, probing questions. We will discuss a variety of questioning styles for your sales tool box. Finishing our section on communication, you'll learn how the senses play a part in how you create a message for your customer.

Behavior plays a key attribute in sales. You can match your customer's behavior if you are able to understand and identify their approach. By being able to identify, you can change your approach on a case-by-case basis. This in turn builds rapport and more sales, making a bigger "ka-ching" of the cash register. The simple and learnable DISC profile will be explained to help better understand the concepts.

Next, we will look at how you start to build up a client base through networking. You'll look at how to call clients and build a strong base to work through.

Lastly, we will discuss time management, which is more closely related to self-management. Once you can manage yourself, you are able to manage the sales and your business.

Now let's get started in putting together a new set of skills that will help you build more sweet sales and find sweet success!

CHAPTER 1

14 ELEMENTS OF A WINNING SALES MENTALITY

More than most other business professions, you win or lose with your mindset. In sales you plan and then execute, not mindlessly flapping in the wind, waiting for the sales prospect to show up. You need to hustle, move quick, think on your feet and act. You need a sales mentality.

In sports the game plan is laid out, the opponent analyzed, players have their roles and run their plays. Then the game begins. As the game progresses, individual performance may dictate the plan. A player may sprain an ankle and sit-out and the back-up player comes in. The game continues with alterations to the plan. There is no ideal world.

Sales plays out the same. The players need to know the basics, like prospecting and creating proposals. When the sales funnel starts to fill, though, be it a simple-sale or a complex-sale, your mindset will determine your performance.

Dr. Jim Loehr scientifically observed in his book *Mental Toughness Training in Sports* and then went on to apply this in business models, showing that the mind can make the difference between winning and losing. If you take two Olympic athletes, you'll find most physical attributes equal. They have trained their body for the trials and tribulations of winning. What Dr. Loehr showed with athletes, especially professional tennis players, is that the time between the points, when the athlete were inside their own heads thinking, evaluating, talking to themselves, that was when the match was lost or won.

Your ability to think and evaluate in a manner that helps you win the sale can be a huge difference in your daily performance as a professional.

I've set out here 14 Elements of a Winning Sales Mentality that you can work on to improve your mindset before going into the sales game. It takes a lifetime of working on these skills and still some days you'll be on your game and other days not. If you find yourself thinking that you miss any one of them, pause for a moment and think about what steps you can take to start building that element, making it stronger. Instant behavior will start to strengthen your mindset. Write down an action you can take and then push to take that action. It's like bodybuilding where you need to consistently work different parts of your body to make it stronger. Some days you may work legs, other days arms and other days other core muscle groups. Each of these elements of sales need to be developed, practiced and grown.

Clarity of Purpose

For over two decades I've taught that salespeople must be clear about what they want. Before you pick up the phone, before you get into the car, before you make a presentation, you must be clear about what you want. Clarity of purpose makes that happen.

In the forefront of your mind, you see what you want. You have the vision and the focus of where you're going.

Great sales people limit their target clients, focus on the main area, know their ratios and how they will work their calendar. Then they execute this with clarity of purpose in their mind's eye. Over and over, a salesperson will sniff out where the deal is. When they sink in their teeth, they hold on without release until the deal is closed. I've witnessed experienced and inexperienced sales professionals alike, who have this clarity of purpose, the drive to narrow in and go for the kill.

One sales guy came in and though he was in training for the first 2 weeks, he was out on breaks and lunch hitting the phone. He made his first sale in 3 weeks while the rest of the class took 2-3 months to complete their first sale.

On the flip side, I've also seen sales people that do double the work, hit all their ratios, do the "right" things, but they miss this clarity and they flounder. They go through the motions. They hit the KPIs, just for the sake of hitting them. They act without clarity of purpose.

In your sales, aim for the single-minded action. If you still lack clarity of purpose, then read success stories of great Olympians and athletes to show you the possibilities.

Time Management

Time management is so important I have a whole chapter on it. You have to know as a successful salesperson how to plan. You need to understand how your energy is directed as it is so important to your success. The time management mindset must be one that you think to yourself. "Will my current action lead to a sale?" A sales person knows what needs to be done and when to do it. They have targets set up and they create the mindset that they will take action and succeed. They look at their ratios and then work to improve their ratios.

Action Oriented

One sales mentor used to call a sales meeting as having a "belly-to-belly" meeting. "You should have two belly-to-bellies a day," he would say. The reason I like this image is it is kinesthetic and relays a sense of motion. Salespeople should have a sense of action, progressing forward, moving things to a conclusion, i.e. a sale. They are often asking themselves, "What next? What will help move this sell along?" The mentality, even for a slow moving, complex sale, is one of action and forward progress.

Because of an action-oriented focus, sales professionals around the globe come off as aggressive. This is just a word that we label action and may have negative connotations. Remove that stigma. Let's look at the dictionary definition of aggressive: "The practice or habit of launching attacks." This is sales to a tee. But rather than hostile or destructive behaviors, it is creative and building. If you move slowly rather than taking immediate action on your client's needs, then you have joined the wrong profession. Dynamic, vigorous, vital, energetic, enthusiastic, live. You should be out singing and shouting your product or services merits from every corner and on top of every mountain. You should be asking for referrals from everyone you meet. To have that enthusiasm, you must also carry a strong, immovable belief.

Strong Belief

First, you need to believe in yourself.

Next, believe in either the product/service and/or the company you represent.

Lastly, you need to believe in your industry, including the value of your product and/or service and specifically to sell the benefits of working with your company.

If the synergy of any of these three fail to work together, then success will elude you. Sales may occur, but they will be hit-miss, up-down and lack the consistency that sales people crave. If you believe in what you're doing, you will evangelize and be unstoppable.

The three beliefs are like a target. The outside ring is the product or service. The next inner ring is your company. The core is the salesperson. You as the salesperson are the core to making the company and the product or service come to life. People relate to people. For example, I may want a computer. In essence, any brand works. Apple carries many devices, some of which may be irrelevant. The salesperson, however, personalizes the experience and can find my needs, and tells me a story that relates the other two rings in the target.

Enthusiasm

The etymology of the word comes from the Greek, meaning "possessed by a god." I love that. When you are in the zone, when the world is working synergistically, when you are enthusiastic, you will sell more. That intensity and excitement will be contagious to your buyer. Enthusiasm most often manifests itself in dynamic sales, friendly chortle and encouraging follow-up calls. We think of the loud, Wolf of Wall Street enthusiasm. However, from my experience, the best salesperson is subtle, with quiet assuredness and a fire-in-the- belly that is humble. It is walking into the office in the morning, without leads and thinking, "I'm going to pick up the phone and help someone today in their work by selling to them." Your possession carries with it a magnet and you'll help others in sharing your belief. As Bear Bryant said, "I think the most important thing of all, for any team, is a winning attitude. The coaches must have it. The players must have it. The student body must have it. If you have dedicated players, who believe in themselves, you don't need a lot of talent."

Desire to Succeed

A sales person will drive an extra mile, make the extra cold call, spend longer on that RFP, do a bit more research on her client, read the client's annual report before walking into the conference, work as many hours or persistent days just to get the job done. The best salespeople like the best athletes, move beyond required action and into the exceptional, whether going through sales training, putting added information in the database, or making more sales calls. They take the one extra step others ignore, forget, or neglect. The great sales person knows that in the sales race, there is only first place or nothing; no medals are awarded for second best sales person, only unemployment checks.

One of my sales teams went out bowling. A new team member had just started. Though we were all novice bowlers, this was her first time. In the first round, as we expected, she threw gutter ball after gutter ball. What I noticed, however, was that walking back to the seats she was muttering, "I'm going to win. I'm going to win" The second round, against all odds, she went from last to first. She took that desire to succeed mentality into her sales and lead the team and ended by becoming the first women sales manager of the organization.

You need to be the salesperson who never says die. Your sheer will may help push through what seem like impossible sales situations. Don't "hope" for a sale to happen, "expect" it to. This self-fulfilling expectation, determination and tenacity creates consistent sales. Experience can sometimes destroy this belief and expectation. After years of experience, we again learn that determination can take the place of naivety. Those are the players you want around you to help you drive forward and use as a model to help you succeed.

I think the best salespeople know their ratios, their sales processes and follow their own system. But on top of that, the best salespeople need to be resourceful and creative. I abhor and run from the salesperson who says the word "can't." When the markets turn, then they will be the first out the door. You need to find ways to gain leads, to find names, to open the door. I'm sure you've heard in your office sales people that say, "I can't get to the decision maker." I know that you would never use that phrase, but perhaps you've heard others say it. Then someone walks up to them and says, "Have you called so-and-so and asked them for the person's name? They play squash together." Wow! That simple. Yes, it can be. The resourceful sales person with the desire to succeed will ask themselves, "What way can I make this happen?" and then start implementing. No excuses.

Responsible for Their Actions

You may not be able to control your environment, but you can control how you react to the environment. You don't blame a poor market, bad customers, or natural disasters. Great sales people see what is in their power to change and are responsible for making things happen. They drive, rather than get driven by what goes around them.

In Tokyo, when the financial crisis hit, Bear Stearns and Lehman Brothers had created a vortex of destruction that pulled many businesses down around them. The average sales person complained about the market, how clients were going under and the impossibility of finding new clients. Many sales people quit, left Japan and went back to their own country or other countries where they felt the environment made sales much easier. However, those with the traits listed here, along with the ability to know what they could control in their environment, made the sales. Some of them worked longer hours, they definitely made more cold-calls, they spent time with existing clients to see how they could help them succeed, they thought outside the box and created networking events for others in their field and they became active in their community to find out how they could help others and in doing so increase their sales. They controlled themselves, the one thing they could control. In your mind-set arsenal, make sure you know your sphere of influence, increase it and focus on what you can control, letting the other stuff fall away.

Driven for Self-Improvement

I think the days of the aggressive, go-getter sales people is starting to wane, even in some of the most aggressive of sales professions. The best sales people desire to improve themselves. Not all action, the modern sales professional stops to take time to read and improve themselves. They listen to others and what the customer has to say, rather than forcing a solution down their throat. They observe and put into practice what they see working with others. Curious to understand their customer's needs, they turn to their customers and ask them how they do what they do. The continually look at their product and service to understand how their customers need and use the product or service. Books, audio programs, seminars, classes and training are a regular part of their regime for both networking and learning.

This continuous improvement includes physical, as well as mental activity. Energy comes from physical well-being. Newton taught that things in motion tend to stay in motion. Great sales people wake up early, go to a work out and then feel the endorphins kick in on a high that lasts the rest of the day. Sometimes they will play a team sport where they can network and compete. Others use the evening to relax and focus, releasing whatever stress has grown from their day of selling. After all, physical well-being is based on discipline and consistency and your health and appearance show the tangible results. Good sales people like simple truths: constituency, discipline and tangible results.

Self-Aware

You need to know your strengths and weaknesses. Self-awareness will help you grow as a sales person. There are two belief systems I often hear: First, "play to your strengths." Second, "improve your weaknesses." I think somewhere in the middle is more accurate. I definitely believe you should know your strengths and always use them as a sales person. If you are excellent at cold-calling and business development, then you use this to open as many doors as possible. If you're weak on closing, you need to learn this element and master it. Closing is a vital sales element. However, you may often find that you can combine the two. For example, ask yourself, "How can I build business development into my closing?" If you are weak on administration, ask yourself, "How will administration build on my cold calling?" Or better yet, "Is there a way to delegate my administration so that I can do more business development?" You soon find that your strengths will absorb your weaknesses and the barriers that you once placed around them, were false. Know your strengths, know your weaknesses and work on both.

Flexible and Adaptable

Though I'm not a paleontologist or scientist, a bit of Darwinian evolution teaches that certain species will become extinct if they fail to adapt to their environment. The cockroach took this to the perfect extreme and continues to thrive!

In 2009, when the markets were crashing, many sales people just couldn't shift their thinking and method of working. They needed to find new prospects, search in different industries and work harder to survive. The salespeople that made the change survived. The weak changed professions or floated from job to job as the company went under or they were fired for lack of results. The results in sales rarely lie. You either make the sale or you don't; you either hunt or kill for your family and the tribe, or you die of starvation. Simple. Along with that desire to succeed, you need to be flexible and adaptable on how you find the results to reach that success. If one method of business development fails, try a different one. If cold-calls fail you, try walk-ins or networking. Keep trying until something works. If success follows, continue to develop the skill while experimenting with other solutions to different challenges. Soon you will have a shell has hard as a cockroach!

Empathy

Even though this is down the list, I rank this element near the top. In sales, you need to relate to your customer. You need to get into your customer's skin, really understand them, feel their problems and challenges from their point of view and then get back into your skin and see how your product or service fits their needs. We all know the adage, "All things being equal, people buy from friends. All things being unequal, people still buy from friends." Friendship and rapport is built from empathy. Think about your own life: you want people to understand you. The primary elements of a salesperson are to ask good questions, listen and empathize. Then you can sell. Some customers buy on price, others on value and still others on convenience. Ask your customer what they want, listen and relate your product or service to their pain. Though you may think like Steve Jobs that you need to show what your customer needs, there is still an element of empathy to understand that the customer may not understand. That's okay too.

Credibility

Educate yourself about your industry, your product and your customer's concerns and from there you start leading the field. When I was selling Business Process Management services to the human resources industry, our sales director had us study for the SHRM (Society for Human Resources Management) the accreditation of Professional Human Resources (PHR). He said that if we were going to sell to HR professionals, we needed to know more and understand their perspective, otherwise we were going to lose on price as a commodity. If you find yourself in an industry that lends itself to commoditization, differentiate yourself by being credible.

Another facet to being credible is to ask yourself, where are the leaders of your field? Are they writing books, giving speeches, setting-up at trade shows, at charity funds, presidents of associations? Ask yourself where you can be a leader. This leads to your credibility. This double approach of learning and leading will do a great deal to help you gain credibility and succeed in sales. It builds synergy.

Energy

Why do salespeople earn more money? They work hard. It's that simple. Having energy and working hard is a hard equation to beat.

Imagine a salesperson who moves slowly, lethargically, meanders to meetings, speaks to clients in a slow drone. A good salesperson? No way!

Though a bit of an exaggeration, we love those salespeople who are quick. Move fast. Make decisions. Have urgency. For this reason, I encourage all sales people to exercise. Become addicted to the adrenalin built from working out. You'll work faster with more energy.

I'm not advocating those fast-talking, used-car type of salespeople. Rather, what I'm talking about is a sales engine that drives every great organization: the group of men and women who go out and build relationships, offer solutions, provide goods, make the cash register ring and drive the global economy. Have energy!

Last Laugh

Lastly, salespeople should have a great sense of humor. Sales is a profession where you hear "no" a lot. You can't take it all that seriously. If you do, you'll quickly burn out. When making a cold-call to the CEO of a building company that excavated swamp land for homebuilders, I called and said, "Hi, I'm selling dinosaur footprints." Needless to say, I was the only salesperson that had called him up saying this. I showed up to his office and presented him and his sons, small plastic dinosaurs and smiled and said, "Like dinosaur footprints, our service helps your company make a footprint in the market." With a smile and a bit of tongue-and-cheek creativity, I closed the sale.

So how many of these elements do you have? Take a moment to check off the ones you have. Rate yourself 1-5. How do you score?

ELEMENT	SCORE
Clarity of Purpose	
Time Management	
Action Oriented	

ELEMENT	SCORE
Strong Belief	
Enthusiasm	
Desire to Succeed	
Responsible	
Driven to Learn	
Mental & Physical Self-Aware	
Flexible & Adaptable	
Empathetic	
Credible	
Energetic	
Sense of Humor	

Now, take a moment and think about it...

1. Personally, what do you consider the 5 most important mindsets for you as a sales person? Explain why.

2. What 5 actions will you take immediately to improve your mind-set? Explain why. Explain specifically how.

3. How will you know when you have succeeded? When will it be accomplished?

CHAPTER 2

INVISIBLE SELLING

In the previous chapter, you saw the mind-set that a salesperson needs to survive, then rated yourself on them and found the ones to take action upon to improve the nucleus of you: the thoughts, which guide your actions.

In this section, you will learn invisible selling: communication skills. Communication means many things, invisible things that are often taken for granted, which is why they are invisible: how a person speaks, the tone of voice, diction, appearance, gestures and many of the ways people communicate without knowing it. As a salesperson, you will start to observe, study, learn human behavior and notice the invisible and use it to your advantage. Some may think this sounds like manipulation, but really over two thousand or so years people called it rhetoric.

Some of what you will learn may be a review but some will be new to you. Go through this portion with an open mind. Observe yourself and others. What you're aiming for is that even if your product or service costs more than the competition, you can still sell more and better. Even in a depression, recession, or frozen market you can still make money.

From the drive-through window at Taco Bell to the woman, who rings you up Saks Fifth Avenue, to the pet-shop owner selling you an iguana, to the consultant helping you install a new ERP system, nothing gives you more power than invisible selling with eminent soft skills.

Imagine for a moment you're at a dinner party with a few close friends. One of your friends introduces you to someone you find attractive. Now imagine to yourself that this good looking stranger listens intently to you, caring about what you say, asking questions about your trip to the Bahamas, your new pet iguana and laughs at all the right times when you talk about your recent visit to Taco Bell.

How do you feel about that person? I would imagine you would forget about all the other people at the party and focus on this wonderful new friend. Most likely you're intrigued. Maybe even captivated when this person speaks, chances are, you would in return listen to them.

Do you see the power of these soft skills? Looking nice, questioning, listening and speaking politely? This stranger, in reality, could be uninteresting and dull, have different hobbies and know nothing about the Bahamas, your pet iguana, Taco Bell, or care one iota. The point is, you don't know! You've been intrigued by this person and want to know more!

In sales, before you add your product/service knowledge, your industry knowledge, or sales skills, you need to first have the unquantifiable invisible selling skills.

When I started out in sales I remember going out on a call with a seasoned professional to visit the vice president of internal audit at Bank of America. My mentor wore a blue, pin-striped suit and had French cuffs and cuff links. His wing tips reflected polished perfection. Though he had only a basic grasp of derivatives, fixed income and reverse floaters, he could speak as an equal with the VP of audit in front of him. The key, I later understood, was that he looked just like an investment banker and when he walked into the office, he could ask questions and listen to the director. Before you can push product or service, you must first look the part, ask the right questions, listen to the answers and ask intelligent follow-up questions.

Here is another example that clearly showed me the importance of invisible selling skills. I was going through a drive-thru restaurant. I started reading the menu and deciding what to eat. No one really expects the best customer service at a fast food drive-through window, but even the barest minimum makes a difference.

After deciding, I tried to start ordering, but no answer came. I sat for nearly two minutes. Finally, I shouted at the drive-thru speaker. "Hello!"

Another sixty seconds of silence. Finally, a voice says: "Wait a sec."

I waited and thought for a moment. I don't mind when someone speaks in an informal, colloquial manner, such as "sec" for "second." I know that if I want highbrow, proper Queen's English with my meal, I'll patronize a restaurant with a white tablecloth and a candle on the table.

What struck me though was the lack of politeness. No "please" or "thank you" attached. Read this and judge for yourself:

"Please wait a sec. Thanks!"

A bit different. Not nearly as flat as, "Wait a sec!"

It doesn't even read, "Thank you," but only "Thanks." With just the simple addition of a politeness, the sentence and selling power, improved tremendously. "Please" and "Thank you" can carry a lot of weight.

That's the point. Even the smallest improvement to soft skills can refine your selling, sometimes making or breaking the sale. It doesn't matter how much you know about a product or how good you are at prospecting or cold calling or what you know about closing. Granted, those imperative skills can make or break you, but if you have them and you're a jerk, then people won't buy from you. It's as simple as that.

So let's get started on improving your invisible soft skills. Whether you're just out of college and in your first sales job or you're a seasoned veteran with the scent of money rolling off your cufflinks, you should still take time to read and learn how soft skills create synergy.

Attitude

Attitude projects your thoughts into action. In a sales person, this attitude needs resilient boldness and strength. You need an energized, positive, can-do attitude. A never-give-up attitude. An enthusiastic attitude. All these we covered in the previous chapter on mind-set. Let's now dive deeper into attitude and what it means in sales.

First, you need to realize that you control your attitude. If someone tells you that you are worthless and will always be worthless and you believe that and start acting worthless, then you live with that choice. You literally self-destruct. You make the choice to accept that attitude. However, if someone says you are worthless and you ignore it because of your bold and strong character and see clearly the path you have chosen to take, then you will continue to pick up the phone. You'll read to improve your skills. You will begin to exceed your numbers and knowing you're excellent, you'll begin to succeed.

A positive example of an external source influencing attitude is when you see someone promoted. After a person is promoted, they often feel a stronger sense of purpose, a deeper confidence and begin to act the part. This was a clear choice that played an influence on the person's thoughts manifest into action. Moving from "assistant" to "manager" may carry no change in a job description, but the title can definitely change a person's attitude.

Self-talk forms a part of this. You need to talk to yourself in a positive manner. There has been a great deal of work in Neural Linguistic Programming (NLP) over the past years and it's a great field to start looking into as it can change a great deal in your life. However, don't confuse NLP with "positive thinking." If you think that being positive alone will raise your sales numbers, then you have another thing coming.

For example, if you walk out to the garden and say, "It's a beautiful garden, it's a beautiful garden, it's a beautiful garden" and you take no action, the weeds will still be there. The tomatoes still die. You must take action. Action creates the momentum. As you take action, you take wrong turns and often meet dead ends. Those side streets make sales a joy, it makes life interesting. Many people though, come down hard on themselves when they meet these challenges. We all make mistakes.

Think back to a time when you screwed something up. You just botched it. You call up your best friend. I guarantee your friend will say things like, "It's okay. You're all right. Just brush it off and keep going. Don't give it any more thought. Learn from it and do better next time."

These words ring of someone who loves you. They give your attitude a boost and help you proceed forward.

On the other hand, what do you usually say to yourself? You might grumble and mumble things like: "You stupid fool! You schmuck! How could you be sooooooo stupid? You'll never be able to show your face again." Your whole body tenses up and you cease to act. We've all been there and done that.

Why aren't we nicer to ourselves? Why not speak nicely to ourselves as much as our supportive friend would? Why not say to ourselves, "It's okay, try again?"

Brian Tracy, in his Psychology of Selling, tells us to constantly repeat, "I like myself. I like myself. I like myself!" Though you may feel this is dripping of cheese and I have to admit, it sounds cheesy, but if you try it, you'll definitely feel the change.

Until you start effective communication with yourself, you won't start it with others, especially customers.

Here is another example. When a baby starts to stand and hold onto the edge of the coffee table or the nearby chair, all the relatives support the baby. They shout, "Come here! Come to your aunt Heather!" The baby smiles takes a step and falls down. What do the relatives do?

"Bad baby!" they shout. "What a bad baby! You'll never walk! What a failure. Give up. Forget it." And then walk off.

No, of course not! They pick up the baby. Smile. Then cheer her along again to take a second chance at walking.

With your attitude and self-talk, you need to give yourself permission to fail, opportunities to learn and grow, many pats on the back and words of encouragement. In sales you hear, "no" a great deal already. Might as well zealously support yourself. Failure already happens most of the time.

Attitude, Part 2: Failure is Most of the Time

The sales game is like baseball. You can fail over 70 percent of the time and still succeed. Think about it. Out of fifty cold calls, I guarantee that most of those people you call will say, in one form or another, "No thanks, I'm not interested." World-class cold callers land one meeting out of twenty-five calls. No great percentages of success.

Over and over and over again, rejection follows you. When a phone call brings a "Yes, I'll speak with you," you jump up and down. "You may have a meeting!"

Same in baseball. You strike out time and time again. Maybe one out of four times you'll actually hit the ball. If you're batting .250, you're doing your job. With so much failure, you need to start with a great attitude and kindness to yourself. No, not just a great attitude, but an attitude of excellence, filled with richness and enthusiasm. You need an attitude that exudes confidence and says, "I am the best."

We like things that seem excellent and out of reach. Sales people, who act just a tad aloof (not too much though), make it much more enticing for someone to do business with them. Someone who says, "People are knocking down my door. I would love to wait for you to make up your mind, but I have another customer willing to pay more." This attitude brings need and want. The more you drive longing into a customer's mind, the more appeal you have.

However, a word of warning: you can't use this if it isn't true. You have to know in your heart of hearts that you can reach someone else who will pay more. If you don't believe it, then the lie will come out in your voice, in your tone. Tell the truth, showing your integrity.

Often, when veteran sales people go out to a sales call with more inexperienced sales people, amazement shows in the beginner's eyes when the veteran asks that "killer question," or a "sensitive question" without any trouble. "I could never do that," says the rookie sales person. "It just would sound forced."

The strong attitude and belief of the great veteran tells them they live at the same level as the person they sell to. By both people working on this same level, they begin to create an aura around them. Granted they may or may not work with each other, yet they both provide value for their work and lives and search for ways to assist each other in a mutually beneficial way.

When you act as if you own the business, as if you own the world, business owners respect you because they find value in your conversation before they have spent a cent. But if you fail to provide, you've wasted their time. You'd better find an attitude where you have value to offer! Information is the greatest value and the better you pass it along, the more value you add.

If you work with a long sales cycle, then you need to have the attitude of persistence. Think of going two years to drive a sale, speaking to many economic buyers, working with government bodies, looking for agreement, negotiation with engineers and managers. You need strong belief to proceed. This happens when you're selling a new system, packaging line, or high-cost item. If you lack the attitude of success through the process, you'll lose the sale to your competition, who has the attitude.

Looking the Part

My first sales job was at the age of 8 going door-to-door selling stationery. I had saved money from cleaning the house and pulling weeds in the yard. My parents funded the rest of my capital. With my $30, I purchased note cards with kittens, pastel colored stationery sets and daffodil decorated writing paper. Then my parents dressed me in my Sunday suit, which consisted of slacks and a tie. Rather than walking around our neighborhood, I went to the upper-class neighborhoods where there were older customers with more money. Knocking on the doors and sporting a big smile, I asked the lady of the house if she wanted to buy some stationery. The grandmotherly women looked down at this cute kid in a suit. House after house bought stationery! My selling ratios were probably the best of my career. Then I told them I would be back next month; month after month, house after house, I sold my stationery at a marked-up price. It was an easy sell and a huge profit, not to mention a great lesson.

First, this wasn't a kid in jeans and a t-shirt. Though most clean-cut, smiling children can melt a person's heart, one in a suit and tie will make them sigh.

As adults, a good-looking suit on a man or woman, with colors that match and a professional aura about them will instantly impress and moreover, their sales will go up!

In any profession, you should dress appropriately. If you go to a doctor, you want her dressed like a doctor, you go to the butcher, you want to see a bloodied apron and for a professional business person (not just sales) you want in a suit. Of course, you need to dress relative to your location and business sector. For example, if you're in Hawaii, tweed would look a bit awkward. In Tokyo, a dark suit is a must. The point being, look at your customer, then dress appropriately and a step up from that. Jeffrey Fox, author of the great little book, *How to Become a Rainmaker*, recommends that you should be the best-dressed person you will meet during the day. "You are letting the customer know he or she is important to you." That is the type of person to make the sale.

Study the chart below.

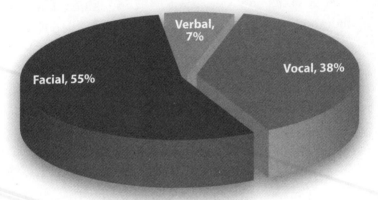

This chart is based on Albert Mehrabian's 1967 study on non-verbal communication. Though there has been much criticism of the simplification of the numbers, it rightly points to the fact that over 55% of how we communicate is visual. We judge people a great deal by how they look. Now you might think that judging a book by its cover is shallow and as children we were taught to refrain. But in the real world, we do it. Half of our communication is body, face, hair, clothes, jewelry and make-up. You may give as many excuses as you want for dressing the way you want, grooming the way you want and accessorizing how you want, but if you want to be world-class at selling, you will hinder your chances of making a sale. To synergize sales, look your best.

If you want to reflect a professional view, then go out and have an image consultant look over your wardrobe. They will tell you what colors look good on you and how you should style yourself. It will pay for itself in less than a year.

One other fact to remember: when you look good, you know it and then you act better. If you act like a million bucks, people treat you like a million bucks and will pay more money for you and your goods and/or services.

Let me give you another example. You meet two financial advisors this afternoon. The first comes in dressed in khakis and a short sleeve shirt, typical business casual. He gives you great advice, you like him. The second advisor comes in dressed in a dark, well-tailored suit and tie, polished dress shoes. He too gives you great advice and you like him. Now all things being equal, which advisor do you think makes more money for their customers? Of course, the one dressed like a professional. Why? Because of our mental conditioning, for better or worse, we trust those who dress as if they have already succeeded.

Some may call me an elitist, a snob or tight stuffed-shirt. I would say, "yes" to all these descriptions. I would also say that you will go further, faster, if you follow the advice of dressing for success.

However, let me expand on this. I think you should also dress for impact. I once went to a vendor conference at Dell. In the room were about 15 sales people. We all wore dark blue suits, white shirts, ties. All of us looked the same in our sales uniforms. Nothing distinguished us from one another nor added any impact. In addition to the rule to be the best dressed person you'll meet today, I also believe you should create a positive impact on your customer. How do you do this? In different ways. In this example, if my sales skills were good enough and my service better than everyone, I might go for an Aloha shirt with my suit. It would make a bold statement that I have confidence and experience and more than a bit of personality. Be professional, but balance this with creating an impact. In the middle, you will find that you have created your persona.

Your Persona

What is persona? A persona is an identity or role that someone assumes, such as a character in a play or a movie. In this sense, a persona would be different than the person you show to your family or friends. All good salespeople create a persona for themselves. Think of your persona for a minute. What kind of character do you draw of yourself? What do you want others to think when they meet you? What do you want them to think when you speak? What do your clothes, body language and manners say about you? And most importantly, what do you want people to say about you after you leave?

Part of sales is a performance, like an actor and to succeed, you need to develop your persona. A professional that exudes understanding, curiosity, success, confidence and all the rest of the characteristics listed in Chapter 1.

For over a decade I was a commercial and stage actor. I would spend a great deal of time in make-up. It was, in part, the hot lights that would make the actor's skin look pale. The makeup compensated for that. I wore costumes that matched the time-period of the play. If I was a prince in the medieval Europe, I needed to make sure I wasn't wearing my digital watch.

Why would you be any less careful in business in general and sales in particular? You need to present yourself as the master of sales, memorize your lines and speak them with feeling and power.

Many sales people come up to me at the seminars I deliver and say, "I want to be more natural. I want to be myself and this just doesn't feel comfortable to me." My answer: "Too bad, this isn't home, your friends, or your family. This is work, your business and in joy you should learn to be the best." I like to add my Gordon Gekko quip, "If you need a friend, get a dog!"

Not only actors, but also athletes prepare their characters in a similar fashion. The athlete mentally rehearses all that they have practiced. Olympians do mental training. Then they fit themselves in proper attire. When you see a linebacker go out on the field, he presents himself in his full gear, mentally charged and ready to play.

When I was growing up, a couple of baseball players stuck in my mind. Part of the reason they stood out was they understood this concept of character.

You may remember the hall-of-famer, Catfish Hunter. Though he got the nickname "Catfish" from a coach, I remember him with the Yankees throwing his stylistic sidearm pitch and his handlebar, catfish moustache. Not only was he good, but he kept the persona going to help his image.

Also watching the Yankees, I loved Bucky Dent. In the 70's, the Yankees were a rough, tough team. But Bucky Dent bucked the trend and was clean-cut and good looking, with his trademark eye black. It was his style and character that made him the best persona on the Yankee's team.

Sales professionals must master character. In a time where people like to dress down, have business casual, we must take our profession up a notch and expect more. Our customers do.

Again, this is relative to your industry and geographic location. But the advice works whether you're in Los Angeles, Denver, Tokyo, Singapore, London, or Sydney. Spend the time to view your industry. Then look at yourself. What are your unique traits that you can develop, expand, grow and perfect when you execute a sale? You're not shooting for the extravagant but appropriate, professional and memorable.

Now, let's take the idea of character one-step further: the experience you offer your customer.

Experience

Experience means to create an ambiance around you or an effect from you and your behavior that impacts your customer, whether it be for good or bad. When you consider how you dress, your script and product or service, you need to consider the experience you give your customer.

Here is an example.

You take your family to Disneyland to have a magical experience. Walking through the streets in front of Cinderella's castle, you see characters from the movies all around you. You're taken back to your childhood, but you're also laughing with your children as they experience Mickey, Pooh, Pinocchio, Buzz Lightyear and a host of others. Each moment, show and ride makes you think of Walt Disney's wise words, "If it can be imagined, it can be created." When you arrive back home you feel as if you've never left childhood and you're humming to yourself "It's a Small World" or maybe "Zipadee Doo Da."

On the flip side you may go to Universal Studios. You jump onto the Hulk roller coaster blasting you from 0 to 60 in less than 6 seconds. Your whole family twists and turns on the Popeye ride and finally find you're soaked! The Spider Man ride makes you feel like him as you swing from building to building through the city. The experience at Universal brings excitement and thrills.

Both Disney and Universal are theme parks with similar rides and concepts. They both compete for your money and time. It's not that one may be better than the other. The "experience" received as a customer visiting the respective park brings you back again or turns you away. When you leave the park with a feeling, that is the "experience."

No matter what you do, you create an experience. One of your tasks, as a sales professional, is to control all the elements that you can, to create the experience you want your customers to have. Of course, not everything can be controlled, any more than you can control everything in a Disneyland or Universal Studios. However, many of the major parts can and should be handled.

One of the most important ideas you and your organization can ask is, "What experience are we selling?" Even if you believe you provide a positive experience when a customer meets you, you need to re-think your position. Everyone will have an experience. How will they remember you? Will they even remember you at all? Will they think of you as professional and slick or as a person with high integrity and speed? A high achiever who fixes problems immediately or will you be that used car salesman, someone the customer doesn't trust and loathes dealing with…that annoying person in a cheap suit, whose breath smells like coffee and cigarettes? Think like a customer. What experience, if you were working with you, would you want to have? Be specific and begin to put actions in place that trigger a memorable experience for your customers.

Take a look at your sales process. Start to document each stage that the customer comes into contact with you, your company and you, from the marketing of your website, to the way you answer the telephone and respond to emails, presentation materials and self-presentation. Each step should be observed, practiced rehearsed. The more steps you control, the better you can assist customers on their unique challenges or on any emergency that arises.

This is a real challenge. As for the immediate cause of our customer's experience, it is difficult to gauge accurately how the customer feels. Within the confines of our office, it is difficult to truly perceive how customers rate our business. Good sales people will ask. Great sales people will listen and adapt appropriately.

To fully understand how you can create an experience for your customers, we need to travel back in time to see how the ancient Greeks created an experience.

Logos + Pathos + Ethos = Gravitas

Logos comes from Greek and in the simplest form translates to "word," though the connotation delves deeper than that. It also contains the means by which an inward thought is expressed. In the Gospel of John, the famous beginning: "In the beginning was the Word and the Word was with God and the Word was God," the Greek for "word" was logos. Over time logos has brought us other words and meanings, such as the word logic. If you think of Logos as a logical aspect of your thoughts to words, that will be enough. In communication, remember, only 7% of your message is communicated verbally. That is, 7% which consists of logos.

Pathos may sound like one of The Three Musketeers, but really it means "emotion." Pathos nowadays also specifies sad emotion, but if you broaden it to strong emotion it comes closer to the true meaning. Advertisements love to use pathos in advertising. Do you remember the commercial for car tires where the baby in diapers crawls over the black tread with a white background? Well what does a baby logically have to do with the tire? Not much! Maybe there is a bit of connotation linking family and safety. But babies make us feel emotion and we remember and feel persuaded.

Advertisers again love to use celebrities in commercials. When you see a celebrity endorsing a product outside of their area of specialty, remember pathos. I remember the Pepsi commercial with Michael Jackson. Michael Jackson would not hold a can of Pepsi. Even though the audience knew that he did not drink Pepsi or directly support the product, Pepsi still made profits from the commercial just by the emotional effect of Michael's fame. That's pathos in action.

Babies, small animals, humor and sex are all *pathos* modes of persuasion. One of the key elements that Jeffrey Gitomer brings out in his excellent book, *The Sales Bible* is the importance of humor. Humor may not work for everyone, but the point of knowing how and when to use it is important component of pathos and a key sales element.

The last element is ethos. Ethos is about the character of the person. Though ethos has given us the word "ethic," ethos and ethic can sometimes fall very far apart. When you meet a person and speak with them and know in your heart-of-hearts if they are good and kind or cruel and bad, this reveals their ethos. Ethos can be amazingly powerful for someone like George Washington or Patton when they need to lead an army, or when leaders like Gandhi and Mother Theresa move the world without a violent action. We may sometimes liken ethos to charisma.

In sales the quickest way to make your ethos emerge is to refrain from selling. "But isn't this a sales book?" you may be asking yourself right now. Of course, but we need to move beyond the step-by-step mode and into something deeper. Ethos drives us to first understand the customer, to know their wants and needs and to empathize. Too often the salesperson will worry about making every sale. This desperation to close the deal disturbs the customer's confidence, lessening ethos and the experience that the customer receives. The secret of this is if you can walk away from the sale, then the customer will work harder to sell themselves; it's human nature to want what one can't have. If you have this inner-strength, then you carry the power of control. The knowledge to know and believe you can sell anytime and anywhere is powerful. That's why many millionaires loose all their money and again make it back again they know they can. That's a strong ethos.

When you synergize the logos, pathos and ethos of your character, your sales skyrocket. If you can then match these 3 with your message, the benefits to your customer and link them to the needs of your customer you then have reached the pinnacle of sales. You'll be driving an Aston Martin and traveling the Riviera first class.

As you work your way around the ideas of Greek rhetoric, realize how important the understanding of these factors are for making up a salesperson's character. As a salesperson you must always work on your character, refining and improving your base. If you are trustworthy and a consumer needs or wants your product or service, she is more likely to buy from you rather than from just someone who tries to push the product.

Your job is to make sure every action, movement, conversation and interaction, matches and enhances the other.

Let's make a distinction for a moment between the differences of character and personality. Personality is a technique we learn after going to a two-day seminar. You can be happy for a week after the seminar by working on your personality and smiling. But your character may still be flawed and annoying.

Character is what the world sees of you. The only way to really jump into working on your character is to study the biographies and autobiographies of great men and women. You need to continually move towards making yourself better, more accessible, more energetic. You'll have a vision of yourself and then step into that vision.

Throughout history, people have worked on their character and taken pride. It was something worth fighting and dying for if one's reputation was marred. Remember Alexander Hamilton died dueling to uphold the honor of his character. You too need to feel such pride and care for your own character.

When you have put together your logos, pathos and ethos, you find yourself pulsating with gravitas.

Gravitas is a weight, substance and manner that holds meaning. A good synonym is dignity. In our casual culture, you need to remember that too much gravitas may be considered, "rigid" or "tight" or "pompous". Before you get the idea that I'm pushing you towards being an old, stiff, conservative codger, let me assure you this is not the case.

One young woman I worked with had a tremendous amount of gravitas. To her friends and family she was a cute, cuddly and kind as a puppy. When this 22 year old, in her first job out of university and the first time in a sales position, walked into the board room of Goldman Sachs to meet with the COO and the VP of Operations, she stood there and controlled the room. When she spoke, people listened to her and trusted what she said. The room was quiet except for her speaking. You could feel her exude power. That's selling with gravitas. She spoke with logic. She contained an emotion and fire and had an approachable, yet aloof manner.

The best way to learn and acquire gravitas is to watch and model others. Another excellent method, as I mentioned above, is reading as many biographies and autobiographies of great people and sales people that you can find. Read from the greats. Also, when you see gravitas in movies study it. For example, watch Alec Baldwin in Glengarry Glen Ross. In fact, I recommend you turn the sound down and study his body language to see how gravitas works without logos. Alec Baldwin's acting radiates gravitas.

Once you've mastered these characteristics, you start to see yourself on equal terms with a business owner. This is vital in selling and you display it when you communicate.

CHAPTER 3

LISTENING: THE MOST IMPORTANT COMMUNICATION SKILL

An acute ability to listen surpasses all other skills as the most important sales skill a person can develop.

However, most people don't listen—especially sales people. Sales people want to rush right in and explain why their product excels everything else in the market. They love to talk. They love to show their knowledge. But this is a moot point if the customer's wants are neglected. Until that is known, you lack the ability to sell them anything.

When you listen to your customer, you affect their impulse to buy. The natural human response to a listening person is to open up more to them and listen to what they may say. It creates bonds that hold people together.

Listen to everything your customers talk about and forego assuming anything:

- What do they like and don't like?

- What do they want and don't want?

- What are their problems and what are the solutions they want?

- What has worked and what has failed in the past?

If you want one thing to help your sales increase rapidly, start listening. You may need a great opening to get your foot in the door, but to build a common interest you start off getting to know people as people, listening to their stories, their lives and their beliefs. Leave your life at the door as it isn't important at this point. Only the story of your character is important. Here are some simple tips to improve listening skills:

- After a person stops speaking, wait 3 seconds. Before you respond, give the person another chance to think, catch their breath and maybe give you another piece of vital information. Let's face it, most of people wait for their chance to jump into a conversation. When the other person speaks, the response starts to build in the mind and they want to jump into the conversation to prove they understand or that they have done something bigger or better. Refrain. If you count to 3, you'll give yourself the chance to ponder on what someone says and show your good manners. As you often hear, nature gave us one mouth and two ears for a reason. Your job in sales is to use your ears. When someone else is speaking, you need to shut up. This can sometimes prove difficult, especially if the other person pauses. But that pause may allow that person to collect thoughts. The silence may also feel uncomfortable and the customer may fill the void with a vital piece of information that you can use to help the customer buy.

- Pay attention. This may seem so simple that we often forget about it. You must be, both in body and mind, focused on what a person is saying and listening to the parts of the main ideas, the emotion that the words contain and any meaning behind the message. Pay attention to the person. Don't look at passing cars or people. Don't turn around when you hear a noise behind you. Don't keep glancing at what is happening behind the person speaking. Don't look at the person's blouse, pants, receding hairline or nostril hairs. Keep eye contact and pay attention. Pretend you work for the U.N and global peace depends on your skill to pay attention.

- Listen for feeling. It's easy enough to listen to a message, but listening to the feeling underneath the message is tough. This is called empathetic listening and is the best way to make sure you understand.

- Respond with a question. Rather than responding with a statement after you count to 3, ask a question.

- Use this phrase: "Tell me more about that." This statement shows (1) you are interested (2) that you are listening and (3) you don't assume you know what the person is talking about.

- Review what the person has just said. Then continue to listen. Draw an outline in your mind's eye of what the person is saying.

- Echo what a person says. "So what I hear you saying is X, Y, Z. Is this correct?" It is a simple technique taught in most seminars. Use it, but don't overuse it.

- Use encouragers. Smile, nod your head, say: "uh-huh," "yes," "sure," "I understand," and "I see," while keeping open body language.

- Tell people you are a good listener. People will believe you and test you out at every opportunity. Then you will need to prove it every time you meet that person.

- Suspend judgment. If I tell you about a friend of mine and say, "He was arrested." What do you think? Are there any images forming in your mind? Are you already distrusting, disliking or, even stronger, hating this person? We are conditioned to respond to people and make judgments. I'm asking you to suspend judgment, rather than closing your mind.

- If a customer says, "Our current vendor is the worst! What a bunch of losers," you need to proceed carefully. Rather than agreeing, ask, "tell me more about that." Keep emotionally neutral. If you agree, then you lose, because the customer will think after you leave the office: "That sales person just bad-mouths his competitors. He is just trying to sell me, I don't trust him." Don't agree or disagree. You need to keep your poker face and listen. After they are done venting, you can say, "That's interesting," and move on into your next question.

- Resist internal distractions. Focus on what the other person is saying. Ignore internal and external noises. We speak around 140 words per minute, but can effectively hear more than 400 words per minute! We tend to fill this gap with chatter from our brain and this distraction gets us ready to jump into any conversation with a response at the first chance! Avoid this temptation. Concentrate on those 140 words as if they sprinkle gold coins into pails. They do!

- Take notes. Most people only remember about 50% of what they hear. Jot down the reminders then fill in later with details.

- Let people tell their story. A great deal of valuable information is revealed in a person's narrative. Save your development and clarifying questions for later. This also gives you a chance to build rapport. Your likability is important.

- Listen with your entire body. Show you're listening - lean forward, keep your arms uncrossed. Use good eye contact and nod in appropriate agreement. Avoid looking at your mobile phone. Pay attention!

- Be aware of personal space. If you stand next to someone, don't stand or sit too close. Also be aware of sitting too far away.

CHAPTER 4

NONVERBAL COMMUNICATION

How you look matters most in communication. Then you need to worry about how you receive and give messages; in short, how you listen and speak. You may neglect to think about listening and speaking, the simple acts that we practice every day, but in sales you need to hone in and perfect your skills.

Consider their importance in an extreme situation of negotiating a peace treaty. If you worked for the U.N. to negotiate a peace treaty between two countries, you would be acutely aware of the environment, your clothing and choose precisely each word and phrase. You would also pay particular attention to everything that goes on around you and listen intently for meaning behind the words spoken. When you were sitting at the table for the negotiation, you would conscientiously plan where to sit, your body language and know the background of all parties concerned. Everything would be planned for success, even down to the pens and paper or possibly on this day, stylus and tablets. When wars and people's lives rest in the balance, you pay attention.

We can all agree that a sales call isn't nearly as important as two countries negotiating a treaty. However, if you consciously hone the skills to this high level, then you'll find much more success than the salesperson who walks into a customer's office without a plan.

As already mentioned, you need to remember everything you do communicates in one form or another; verbally or non-verbally it provides an experience. The question you need to ask yourself, "Is everything I'm communicating congruent?" In other words, do your hand gestures match your eye movement, do they match your mouth and if you smile or not, does it match your suit, your wedding band, your shoes and your socks? You may consider this excessive, but all that you present to your customer needs to present the message you want.

This is so important! Every part of your presentation represents you and your service/product like a holographic image. You are a walking commercial; the client observes the product and service through the lens of you and again, all things being equal, if people trust and like you and believe in your communication, they will buy from you. Yes, this is subtle and subliminal and that is what keeps your character intact.

Have you ever watched a movie where a little something was wrong? For example, in Fear and Loathing in Las Vegas, a movie about Hunter S.Thompson, there is a subtle mistake. Thompson was a writer in the early 70s and this movie was supposed to take place in 1971. On the television showing war footage, there are M1 Abrams tanks, which were not built until 1978. In movies we've all experienced these minor mishaps. They shake us out of the dream.

The same holds for making a sales call. You want your customer mesmerized. You want them to think of only your product or service and that product/service is really just a continuation of you.

For example, if you walk into Merrill Lynch, you immediately recognize the difference from Morgan Stanley. They both classify as top-tier American investment firms, but the people and environment feels totally different. Again, remember the example above of Disneyland and Universal Studios.

These minor details will make you totally different from your competitors. You will have all the class of a millionaire and it will make your feel successful and your communication style will fall into place.

Nonverbal Messages

When you listen attentively, you also need awareness of the nonverbal messages you send. Start to make nonverbal communication a hobby. Observe what people do with their hands and face and their posture. Watch for the differences between doctors, lawyers, politicians, corporate chief executive officers and great salespeople. Observe closely facial expressions, body movements, gestures and posture. Watch the facial expressions that people make to express emotion, both good and bad.

Next, take a look at personal attributes such as appearance, including all options that communicators use to change their looks, such as make-up, hairstyles, clothes and jewelry. Take note of how people speak, the tone of their voice when they agree or disagree. What vocal cues do they make for non words, like "ummm" and "yes, yes"?

Another important nonverbal to watch is touch such as a handshakes, hugs and pats on the back. This is important from culture to culture, place to place. A weak handshake says one thing, a strong one another. In Japan, people tend not to shake hands or touch.

Masterful negotiators and teachers use physical environment to manipulate available space. The distance from or proximity to other people and territorial control are also extremely important. Your awareness of how you control them can win or lose a deal. I had a sales call at PLM, a software vendor. A manager walked us into a meeting room where the tables were set up in a U shape for training. He sat at one end of the U and my colleague and I sat on the other. In about 30 seconds I could see that no rapport would take place because of the distance. I took my bag and notebook to where the manager was sitting. He felt surprised, but we could quietly speak together. The physical distance bridged helped to literally bring us closer together.

As mentioned, clothes also play a huge part in what we do. Think for a moment how important police and military uniforms are for communicating authority.

As we have said, professionally dressed business people project success and credibility. Poorly dressed individuals transmit messages of failure and a lack of credibility.

Let's take a deeper look at body language and how it communicates. Every day, people unintentionally convey nonverbal signals by their facial expressions, gestures and body postures. Linguists have catalogued 135 distinct gestures and expressions of the face, head and body. Eighty of these expressions were face and head gestures, including nine different ways of smiling. These gestures and expressions provide insight into the attitude of the originator.

For example, people telling falsehoods will touch their mouth or involuntarily blink. A lie can be seen at the corners of a person's mouth. Crossed arms or legs may display a negative or withdrawn attitude. Hands folded behind the neck or head often show power or authority.

Because involuntary nonverbal communications represent unplanned physical responses, this communication form tends to particularly reveal more honest communication than verbal messages.

Nonverbal communication can be controlled by a knowledgeable sales person and if they are watching, they are able to watch the buyer. You need to interpret nonverbal messages as part of the overall communication system. Typically, an individual nonverbal message is difficult to accurately interpret in isolation because most messages have several possible meanings. For example, a yawn might indicate a lack of interest, physical fatigue, or both; and rapid eye blinking might indicate deceit or just poor fitting contact lenses.

A nonverbal message is easiest to interpret when consistent with other communications that are simultaneously received. For example, you would be more likely to interpret someone touching their mouth as "dishonest" if the person avoids eye contact. Watch to see that messages correlate so that you interpret accurately.

Eye communication also creates immediate nonverbal impact. As shown, much of what we communicate is nonverbal. Eye contact literally connects mind-to-mind because your eyes present the only part of your central nervous system that contacts directly with another human being. When you fail to make that mind-to-mind connection, it matters very little what you say. As a sales professional, this is vitally important.

Remember to make eye contact and not just look at someone's face. When you meet with a group, look at each person for three to five seconds. Exercise particular attention to eliminating rapid and distracting eye movements. Survey your listeners for a few moments before you begin speaking. Maintain your eye contact, but don't try to stare them down. When you sell, you look someone in the eye to tell them non-verbally that you speak the truth.

Another way we communicate non-verbally is with gestures and smiles. When you communicate do you display enthusiasm? Excitement? Do you speak with conviction and passion? Does your listener want to know not just what you have to say, but how you really feel about it.

Open gestures and a warm smile do more for effective sales than almost anything else. Your smile dominates your listener's impression of you as you communicate. A smile shows not only on your mouth but also in and around your eyes. It demonstrates openness and likeability. Smiles are contagious and create endorphins in the body making people feel good. What a super powerful sales tool!

If you are the type of person that has nervous gestures, such as picking your nails or fiddling with pens, you need to stop. This simple habit can be the difference between a sale and a fail to sell. When you are selling you want the customer to concentrate on you. When you are using natural, open and controlled gestures, you find yourself able to express your thoughts more fully and freely, express openness and emphasize points of importance. All this can translate into more sales.

Now let's look at postures. People make a lot of assumptions about you in the first few seconds after they meet you. Assumptions about attitude, confidence, competence and even rank and position. Many people have posture habits that undermine trust and convey a lack of self-assurance. Even if you inwardly feel confident, poor posture will invariably communicate a lack of poise and confidence to your listener because that's their first impression.

When you are out selling, stand tall and erect. Like the old mothers of long-gone days told their children, "Stand tall, shoulders square, back straight, stomach in." If you have the habit of leaning a bit forward, you will also be "psychologically" forward as well. When standing in a group, lean just a bit forward on the balls and toes of your feet. You'll see that such a position will bring you literally more forward.

Lastly, the tone of your words can immediately involve your listener with a strong, energetic presence. If you open up the conversation with a great deal of energy, you'll make an impact that the customer will always remember. If delivering a formal presentation, start with energy. Feel enthusiasm and passion when you speak and it will show. If it helps, imagine that you are Tony Robbins!

The benefit of speaking with energy is that it also keeps your listener's energy up. You can get more of your concepts and ideas across when you have the interest and involvement of the buyer and it's more fun too. Lastly, high energy also reinforces other good communication habits, like eye contact and body movement.

Body Language Application

To summarize, in sales, you use your knowledge of body language in several ways.

As you prepare for your client call, you should briefly review key elements of body language.

- Exhibiting positive attitudes will make you more believable.

- Exhibiting negative attitudes will hinder a sale.

- A questioning look by a team member as you make a statement may bring your credibility into question.

BODY LANGUAGE EXAMPLES			
Positive			
- Hands in pockets with thumbs out - Hands on lapel of coat - Steeple fingers or hands - Good body posture– squared shoulders and a straight back - Hands on hips	- Tilted head toward speaker - Sitting on edge of chair - Upper body leaning - Eyes focused on speaker	- Peering out over eyeglasses - Chin cupped between thumb and fingers - Putting hands to bridge of nose - Stroking chin	- Rubbing hands together - Sincerely smiling - Frequent nodding of the head
Negative			
- Frequent eye blinking - Hand covering mouth while speaking - Frequent coughing - Looking away while speaking - Quick sideways glances	- Arms crossed high on chest - Crossed Legs - Pointing an index finger at another person - Hands in pockets - Constant fidgeting	- Chewing on a pencil - Frequent coughing - Biting fingernails - Tightness of jaw - Rubbing back of neck - Drawing eyebrows together	- Eyes looking elsewhere - Head in hand - Sloppy or informal body posture - Preoccupation with something else

- Your use of positive body language should strongly support your position.

- When you observe your customer, you can gain greater insight into his attitude.

- If a customer appears negative, you might question for more information.

- Remain "switched-on" to what is going on around you with high-sensitivity to body language and facial gestures.

Personal Attributes Affecting Sales

One of the things you can't change much is your personal attributes. Your looks, your height, hair or lack of it, eye color, nationality. All of these things you're born with. However, you need to be aware of the effect that your physical appearance may have on nonverbal communication. Awareness may permit you to build on your natural advantages. Awareness of any natural disadvantage may also be even more important and switched to an advantage. Though we should not judge people only on physical appearance, in selling, it is a key to understanding yourself and your customer. Let's face it, none of us are perfect. But it's good to know what your customer may be thinking about you, so that you can use it to your advantage during a sales call.

Research has found that:

- Physical attractiveness affects the way you perceive yourself and the way others perceive you.

- Keeping yourself looking in top-shape leads to more sales because people buy more from attractive people. They also land better jobs and have more self-esteem and social power than unattractive people.

- Attractive, well-groomed people receive preferential treatment in the initiation and development of interpersonal relationships.

- People perceive taller men and women as more dominant than shorter men and women.

- People also perceive tall females as even more dominant and smarter when they accompany shorter males.

Though you can't change your height, you can change your posture and wear clothes, such as stripes, that emphasize your height. For shorter men, refrain from pants with cuffs. For shorter women, wear heels.

Body Type:

- Generally, people believe that athletic looking people demonstrate more assertiveness and self-reliance than people with other body types.

- In contrast, people believe heavier, less athletic looking people exhibit more laziness and show more dependence than people with other body types.

- Skinny fragile looking people personify suspicious, nervous and pessimistic characteristics.

The point to remember is that everyone displays something with their body-type that may communicate some positive and negative connotations. As a salesperson you need to know this and use it to help you present yourself and sharpen how you read others.

Personal Grooming

We will end this section on invisible selling with a word about personal grooming. General grooming, especially poor grooming, can have a profound affect on how others identify with you. Do not allow poor personal grooming, (such as uncombed hair or an unshaven look) which detracts from your appearance and communicate unfavorable nonverbal messages about you or your product. Remember, that if you look good, you will generally:

- Feel better

- Perform better

- Be perceived better by others

If you've not read a book on dress, then I encourage you to do so. Make sure your clothes are well tailored for your body. If you have little money to spend on clothes, spend a bit more on accessories. A good watch, necklace, tie, belt, shoes will help accent an outfit and make the overall appearance look good. Cologne and perfume should be used sparingly. Women would also do well to take updated classes on applying makeup. Many women learned to put on makeup in junior high or high school and may have changed styles appropriate to their age and position. Also, styles change. Every few years, make sure you take a look at clothes, makeup and hairstyles. I also encourage you to have your colors professionally analyzed to know what clothes bring out the brightness in your skin and eyes. It feels great to look your best.

CHAPTER 5

EFFECTIVE QUESTIONING

We have described nonverbal communication skills, effective listening, now let's start looking at the part of the equation, the part where you actually get to speak: asking questions. The person who asks the questions controls the conversation. Salespeople often think that if they can speak over or out-speak the customer, they will make the sale. With today's sophisticated buyer, just out-talking the buyer won't make the sale.

The ability to ask questions and understand the customer's need is often overlooked. By learning to ask questions, uncovering evidence like a detective, you will instantly increase your earning potential. In fact, over the 20 years I've trained sales people, I encourage them to read murder mysteries, especially Agatha Christie, as an excellent model of how to uncover facts and make the sale. For that reason, she is listed in my recommended reading for salespeople.

To start off, let's look at different types of questions. Questions come in a variety forms. Good lawyers know this and are taught how to ask these questions effectively.

Unfortunately, "Sales" as a topic is not taught in our schools. You need to learn how to use these different types of questions when appropriate and to avoid them when not appropriate. One of the best books on effective question remains *SPIN Selling.* Also, notice that some sentences below are statements that allow the customer to speak, but technically lack the interrogative nature of using a question and instead use "Tell me about..." which can be a very effective way to have a client open up to you.

Open Ended

Examples:

- Who? What? Where? When? How? Why?
- "What benefits are you seeking to derive from product/service such as ours?"
- "Tell me...about your business."
- "How is your procurement done?"
- "What do you hope to gain by our service?"

Open ended questions remain the cornerstone to great sales. They allow the customer to open up and tell their story. When the buyer is involved in the conversation, they feel ownership in the process.

Also, asking questions encourages people to discover things on their own. As psychologists and learning professionals tell us about adult-learning, the ability to talk through ideas and self-discover an idea, impacts the learning process. This information can powerfully translate into sales if you understand your ability to educate your prospect on your goods or services and how it can effectively impact their life and business. To tell someone a fact may help them understand logically. If you want to really effect the prospect, to turn up the pathos in your sales techniques then an excellent open-ended question starts this process. Lastly, as will be covered in a later chapter, when you start a dialogue, the other person's behavioral style reveals itself, which you can use as the sales process unfolds.

Developmental Questions

Examples:

- "Tell me about your experiences with other products like ours."

- "Why did you want to find out about our services?"

- "What discourages you about your current provider?"

Development questions start to narrow in and focus on exactly why the client needs your product or service. They explore why they spend the time to meet with you and reveal ways that your product or service can specifically impact them. These will often be follow-up questions after you have listened to their narrative from your open-ended question above. Or if the prospect starts to wander away from what is positive about your product or service, it begins to bring them back to the line of questioning you'd like to cover.

Clarifying/Probing Questions

Examples:

- "What exactly do you mean by customer service?"

- "How did you measure success with your last vendor?"

- "What impact can our product have in your business?"

- "When you say, 'troubles,' what exactly do you mean?"

- "How much is 'a lot?'"

The value of these questions is that you start to understand what the prospect thinks. You now seek feedback, an explanation, or more detail about your product and service and how it fits into what you're doing. It also starts to reveal relevant strengths and weaknesses, even in areas they wish to hide.

Low Order (Open/Closed)

Example:

- Did you have any problems getting here?"

- What are you doing this weekend?"

- How are you?"

As simple as these may sound, it is immensely important to know how to make small talk. These sorts of questions are unthreatening, useful ice breakers. They can get your client to talk. These types of questions, which are easy to answer, build up a questioning and answering pattern between you and your potential buyer. Use them effectively to start the buyer opening up, revealing themselves to you and understanding that they will be doing most of the speaking.

Closed Questions

Examples

- "Are you the decision maker?"

- "How long have you worked with them?"

- "How many employees do you have?"

In *SPIN Selling*, as Neil Rackham and Bob Kalomeer point out in their research, a good sales professional knows when to use closed questions. In my experience, most sales people ask closed questions without meaning to. When they do, it closes down the conversation. However, an experienced sales person who knows how to selectively ask a yes/no question at precisely the right time, can narrow in and focus their buyer's answers, better directing the conversation. Make sure when you are asking a closed question, you intentionally do so to nail down a point to a definite "yes" or "no" answer.

Fantasy

Examples:

- "Suppose...?"

- "What if...?"

- "Imagine you were in charge of operations. What would you want to see done?"

This line of questioning tests creative, lateral-thinking abilities and reveals thought processes. Also, by asking fantasy questions you can begin to help the buyer picture different possibilities and scenarios with your product or services. If the buyer sees the possibilities and begins to literally imagine them in the mind's eye, then there is conception of how to directly use what you're selling. For that reason, stories and testimonials remain powerful tools in the selling arsenal. When you tell a story, you're using fantasy. When the buyer listens to your story and how others have used your service, she begins to put herself into the story and imagines using your service just as others have previously done. Fantasies hold strong selling force. Use them.

Other Forms of Questioning

Outside of these types of questions, I'm listing below some other types of questions that over the years I've heard sales people ask. In general, these questions styles should be avoided and replaced with questions that are better thought through. The questions below show a lack of logic, planning and consideration, generally reflecting poorly on the salesperson.

Assumptive

Examples:

- "You'd like to avoid legal problems?"

- "It sounds like you've used many companies. Presumably you'd be happy to try our services?"

These questions are called "logical fallacy" questions, or what is commonly called, "a loaded question." The most famous, "Tell me, when did you stop beating your wife?" is a question that assumes the person beat their spouse in the first place. Most of the time, questions like the examples above make too big a leap and lead a person to think you haven't been listening properly.

Broad Questions

Examples:

- "What about your school days?" (Is this relevant to the conversation?)

- "How about operations?" (*Which part of operations?*)

- "How has it affected operations the past decade?" (*A decade? how about 12 months?*)

Questions like these are confusing and may well generate a vague answer or a direct counter question. They show fuzzy thinking on the part of the salesperson.

Leading

Examples:

- "I suppose you have troubles with your current provider?

- "Didn't you have trouble with your last vendor?"

You have probably seen court scenes in movies where the lawyer stands up and objects to the examiner leading the witness. These questions are doing exactly the same to the buyer, by leading then to answer with what you want to hear and not necessarily the truth. When a sale is made on the basis of such questioning, troubles come from after sales service or setting the wrong expectations.

Multiple Questions

Examples:

- "What hobbies do you have, how do you enjoy them and which is your favorite?"

- "Since you started using your vendor, have you had troubles and what were they and how did you solve them?"

This type of questioning is one of the most common that I see new salespeople make. They find themselves in a client meeting, a bit nervous, unsure what to ask and rather than using notes and having a plan of questions, they blurt out all the thoughts that reach their tongue. Most of the time, the salesperson will only get part of the question answered, while the rest is ignored or forgotten. The other challenge is that the buyer usually sits there in confusion, wondering what to answer first.

For and Against Preconceived Notions

Often when we go into a situation, we have a sense of how the conversation will play out. We carry with us preconceived ideas on how a person will answer based on our belief system, rather than going into the situation with an open mind, ready for anything. The point to remember is that you must treat each communication situation as new and unique. As William Boast writes in *Masters of Change*, "You need to suspend closure." Below are some good and bad examples of using prejudging, stereotyping, contrast effects, halo and horns effects.

The following will guide you in helping to suspend closure. Closure often comes when we question based on what we have seen from people around us. Rarely do we conscientiously think through and develop our questioning style. As sales people whose main tools are communication skills with questioning being among the foremost. So just as a hammer is a standard tool for a carpenter, we need to learn, practice and develop in order to shift our style when needed. It's important to learn to use each style and beware of any that you use too often.

One of the easiest styles you can see with young salespeople is prejudging without all the necessary information. They go in, find out that the client is in the market and then without follow-up questions, start selling or rather, pushing their product. On the positive side, however, this allows the salesperson to know a bit about a person before going into a meeting. For example, if you are going in to meet with the Chief Financial Officer, your questioning style may be heavily geared towards numbers and facts. You are prejudging the person, but in this case it is a starting point, not an ending. When we go into Behavioral Selling later, you will have a chance to see how understanding of behavior will assist you.

The most common way to go into a situation with a closed mind is to base your thinking on a stereotype. For example, I watched, at a cosmetic counter, a sales clerk. She started asking questions to an older women based on her own purchases of foundation for herself, with the obvious intent to sell age cream, or anti-wrinkle cream, or some other such product. But in fact, the woman was there to buy cosmetics for her granddaughter. Such a simple stereotype can cause many salespeople and companies to lose the sale. She would have done a much better job to go into the situation asking questions.

However, sometimes it is very useful to stereotype people to save sales time. If you are selling to a young person, you may skip many questions reserved for an older customer, for example. After 15 years in the recruitment industry, I find that some stereotypes hold-up over business types. Accountants tend to be more introverted, marketing professionals are more open, human resources professionals speak more about people. These are generalizations and stereotypes, but as a salesperson, they again help give color to your questioning style. For an accountant, you may start your questions more reserved; for a marketing person more small talk. As the questions draw out more about the person, your style will grow more personalized.

Assumption questioning is a style of jumping to conclusions, making your mind up on evidence you assume to be there, though no information backs up that information. This style is often used in closing a person, for good and bad effects. "So when would you like your product delivered?" though the customer hasn't agreed to buy. Or, "How will you use our service?" This assumes that the customer will buy your service in the first place.

Contrast Effect is where your style of questioning puts a negative and positive together that affects the answers. For example, if you just came inside from a cold storm and your fingers are cold and you place them under lukewarm running water, it feels very hot. You can be (wrongly) swayed by contrasting and must be aware of dangers of first impressions; decide on facts. For example, you may ask questions that greatly push on the negative aspects of a competitor, to try and make your service seem much stronger. But when this questioning style is used alone, it lacks the strong logical impact needed for the customer to buy your product. A long stream of questions explaining why a certain make of computer crashes, loses data, gets viruses and is generally unreliable, does not make the one that is being sold a better piece of hardware. However, when used sparingly, such a contrasting effect can strongly impact and sway your buyer.

The Halo Effect is fairly well known. This is when the buyer enjoys similar interests with you or has a similar personality, which you immediately empathize with and can mean you ignore everything negative. For this reason, your questioning style tends to be along a positive stream, emphasizing friendly possibilities, missing out on core issues, problems and challenges that the customer may be facing. A strong rapport may have been built, but the needs of the buyer are forgotten.

In contrast, the Horns Effect is the reverse of above. You are swayed by one factor, no matter how irrelevant, which sets your mind against the individual to the point that you can ignore everything positive.

For example, if you are selling an accounting ERP service to a CFO of a large corporation and you both have worked at the same multinational accounting firm, your questioning style would emphasize how much you have in common and how much you share. Your questions may lack the follow-up questions needed to understand the true challenges that the CFO and the corporation are facing. Whereas, if you came from a competitive accounting firm, you may ask questions that illuminate and highlight all the mistakes the CFO has created because she came from the competitive firm.

In conclusion, all these styles are neither good nor bad, but the proper use brings power to your questioning. You need to know when and how to change your style based on your customer's needs. Many sales people can naturally change between the styles and know how to shift from one to another. Others may not. Your job is to practice these different styles, learn when they bring the desired effect and understand how they draw the customer out and lead them towards the purchase of what you are selling.

CHAPTER 6

SPOKEN COMMUNICATION

Now you can begin to build upon your new abilities. You have prepared yourself and prepared your questions and you know how to actively listen to the answers; you are now in the position to improve your speaking techniques. These communication tactics can quickly enhance your ability to build rapport with a customer. I also feel that they are important, because by mastering how you use your voice and words, you cease to detract from the sales meeting. Just like when you watch a movie and are lost in the fiction of the moment, the action, the drama, the story but sometimes you witness an anomaly, such as the microphone or that the actor's fake moustache looks incredibly fake, so it wrenches you out of the performance and into reality. The point of selling is for the customer to focus on themselves - their needs, wants, desires, problems and how your product and or service answers those needs, wants, desires and problems. If your speaking tone, pitch and speed can help rather than hinder your sales, then you should take time to really learn these invisible communication techniques.

First, your voice helps you establish rapport. When you match the pace, pitch, timbre and inflection of someone's voice, you start to build a mirror with the person in the same way as body language does. You'll find this especially useful in your dealings on the telephone, but in a face-to-face situation, using your voice and body language in harmony creates a tremendous effect. With your voice, you use various tools at your disposal to make a desired experience. I've seen outgoing and lively sales guys go in and speak to a quiet, somber accountant and lose the sale just based on this mismatching. In the same vein, I've seen quiet salespeople go and speak to gregarious HR customers and lose the sale. People like buying from similar, like-minded people. The salesperson should be like the person and speak like the buyer, with a bit more knowledge so as to educate, consult and solve problems.

Here are some voice qualities to work on as a professional salesperson:

- Pace: This relates to the speed at which you speak. Try to match the pace of the client's delivery from the start. Not only will this help build rapport, but the rapport will allow you to inject a sense of urgency and importance into your sales message.

- Pitch: This is how high or low your voice sounds. The lower your voice, the more serious and professional you sound. The higher your voice, the more enthusiastic, but possibly lightweight, you will sound. Learn to vary the pitch of your voice for maximum effect. Use your breath to best effect with deep, diaphragmatic breaths. When you are nervous, you tend to have a more shallow breath, which in turn causes higher voiced pitch. Customers rarely like buying from a nervous person, as there is a definite lack of trust.

- Timbre: This is the resonance and power of your voice. Better than speaking loudly, clearly project your voice. This makes you sound more confident and the message appears more powerful. Imagine your voice moving outward, bouncing off the front wall; this is projection.

- Inflections: This relates to how you phrase and emphasize words. Do not attempt to mimic your clients, reflect them. If they tend to talk in short sharp sentences, then do the same. The closer your voice and speech patterns match theirs, the more likely it is that you will establish rapport.

Words and Non-words

If you want to make your message charged and energetic, build a strong vocabulary. On the other hand, weak words and the bad habit of non-words quickly drain the energy from your communication. A non-word is the use of such sounds as "um," "er," and "uh."

As a salesperson, you need to explain your services adroitly and expertly describe the advantages. Think with laser-like precision. English is one of the most flexible languages in the world, which gives you the ability to take a single thought and express it in virtually hundreds of ways. With a well-stocked vocabulary at your disposal you can speak with precision, with subtle shades of meaning, with energy and most of all with the ability to reflect the tone and feeling of your customer.

By concentrating on acquiring a large vocabulary, then bit-by-bit, your progress will pay off and your dependence on weak jargon will dissipate. All of us use a great deal of jargon in our work. When you work with a customer, make sure you never assume their understanding.

In comparison, non-words destroy communication faster than a poor vocabulary. "umms" and "ers" distract the listener's ability to concentrate on your meaning. Remember the school days where you had a substitute teacher who continually said, "umm" and you and your friends started counting them?

To combat this bad habit, record yourself on a sales call. Count the non-words you use. You will probably wince a lot as you listen, but you will also become more aware. That awareness will help you control the non-word habit.

Start to replace your non-words with something more powerful: silence. As mentioned previously, you need to feel comfortable in silence. People respond to silence. Your ability to feel comfortable in silence will give you a great advantage when asking questions.

One of the best ways to remove non-verbal language is to join Toastmasters International. When you use an "umm" or an "er" a bell or buzzer rings. Such Pavlovian methods soon cure you of bad verbal habits.

Humor

Humor creates a special bond between you and your listeners. It's virtually impossible to dislike someone who makes us laugh and helps us enjoy ourselves. Don't tell jokes. Leave comedy to the comedians. Fun is better than funny. Your goal is not comedy, but connection, creating an atmosphere of fun, friendliness and openness. Find the form of humor that works for you. If jokes don't work for you, what does? Perhaps you can use stories and anecdotes. However, be wary of using sarcasm!

Now, Think About It...

List 5 ways you can improve your communication skills. Explain how you will put them into effect.

1. _____

_____

_____

_____

_____

2. _____

_____

_____

_____

_____

3. _____

_____

_____

_____

_____

_____

4. _____
_____
_____
_____
_____

5. _____
_____
_____
_____
_____

Now, Think About It...

In selling, how can you improve your communication skills right away? What specific actions are you going to take to improve your communication skills? In what ways will it improve your sales skills? How will you know when you have improved on these skills?

Language and the Senses

Although the least important factor, in terms of the percentage of communication, the words you use do still carry a tremendous amount of weight. The language you use conveys far more than its face value would suggest. It reflects the way you think and it highlights the way you perceive the world. As a salesperson, it is important that you use precise words and style of language, sometimes down to a subliminal level. If you miss this point, you will sometimes create discord, even controversy when communicating with customers.

Sometimes, you may stray from a conversation and wonder why there was discord resulting from the communication. There was no disagreement, per se, just a subtle uncomfortable feeling. This may be due to the use of the senses.

> Man: Do you see how this chair would look better in the corner over there?
>
> Women: I hear what you're saying, but I would feel better to have it near the window.
>
> Man: I see what you mean. We could have a look.
>
> Women: Do you feel comfortable with this change?
>
> Man: Sure. I see no reason not to.
>
> Women: I hear what you're saying. Are you okay with it, then?
>
> Man: Yes.
>
> Women: Okay, then we'll try.

There is nothing wrong here and agreement is had by both parties, but there is hesitation between the two.

As Suzette Haden Elgin explains in her seminal book on communication, *The Gentle Art of Verbal Self-Defense*, we use three main ways to perceive the world and tie those perceptions to language:

Visual: seeing the world

This person speaks in terms of sight:

- "Do you *see* what I mean?"

- "Try to *imagine*..."

- "Let's put it into *perspective*."

Auditory: hearing the world

This person speaks in terms of sound:

- "How does that *sound*?"

- "That rings a *bell*."

- "I *hear* what you are saying."

Kinesthetic: feeling the world

This person speaks in terms of touch:

- "I need to *touch* base with you."

- "Let's get to *grips* with it."

- "How do you *feel* about that?"

These modes of perception that you constantly use in speaking tells the other person a message, without directly communicating them. Listen carefully to which words the person is using and which modes she uses. Don't jump to conclusions based on one or two words. Take your time and listen for themes and styles. By not using these modes you won't necessarily hurt your communication, but in sales it is attention to detail in every facet of your communication that will give you the edge.

Now, Think About It...

Looking at the sensory-specific words below, decide which words apply to each mode of perception: Visual, Auditory or Kinesthetic. Some are tricky and may be in more than one category.

1. See		11. Sound	
2. Listen		12. Impact	
3. Move		13. Tell	
4. Touch		14. Scan	
5. Ask		15. Frame	
6. Sing		16. Rough	
7. Stare		17. Watch	
8. Color		18. Angry	
9. Speak		19. Visualize	
10. Grab		20. Tune	

Look at the following statements (1) Write down the communication mode the person is using, Visual, Auditory or Kinesthetic (2) Write down a possible response to that person. This may seem simple, but many of my students get caught out on this.

1. "So far I like what I see. What would you recommend for my company?"

- Mode:

_____

_____

- Response:

_____

_____

———————————————————————————————

———————————————————————————————

2. "I'm excited about your proposal, however, I'd like to get a feel for how the cost will impact the employees."

- Mode:

———————————————————————————————

- Response:

———————————————————————————————

———————————————————————————————

———————————————————————————————

———————————————————————————————

3. "That's a good point. I'd like to see some more specifics."

- Mode:

———————————————————————————————

- Response:

———————————————————————————————

———————————————————————————————

———————————————————————————————

———————————————————————————————

4. "Can you walk me through the implementation process again?

- Mode:

———————————————————————————————

- Response:

_____

_____

_____

_____

5. "I'd like some concrete evidence of your unique selling points."

- Mode:

_____

- Response:

_____

_____

_____

_____

6. "I've heard a lot of good things about your company. Monique Kirkendall at Califfa said she'd had excellent service."

- Mode:

_____

- Response:

_____

_____

_____

_____

CHAPTER 7

BEHAVIOR PROFILES AND SELLING

If you have never done one of the several Behavioral Profiles, such as DISC, then now might be the time to research and try one out. Not only is it an excellent way to learn more about yourself and others in your office, it also helps you understand your customers and how to adjust your behavior when interacting with them.

Nowadays there are many effective profiles you can use. I recommend staying with "Behavior" profiles, rather than "Psychometric," "Personality," or some IQ/EQ profile. The reason for this is simple. You can change your behavior. You rarely change your personality. What you want to see is the behaviors that dominate your actions, how to recognize dominate behaviors in others and how to appropriately modify behavior in any given situation.

It is natural for us to change behavior in situations. We may act one way with our friends and another way with our family. One way with a close friend and a totally different way with our spouse.

Also, it is important to remember that profiles only help you strategize when you meet a customer. Each person is unique and different. The benefit of profiles is that they give you a new way of looking at your customer and finding better ways to communicate with them.

For simplicity, I'll take you through the DISC "types." I like DISC for a couple of reasons. First, because it has been around so long, there are many studies and a lot of theory to back up the profiles. Second, because it is well known and widely accepted, the profile tends to be easy to acquire and administer to sales teams. Lastly, and for me the most important aspect, the explanations are simple. Sales people want something quick, tangible and effective rather than convoluted theory. As a sales manager, DISC answers those needs.

Here are four generic profiles. You can begin to identify yourself in these profiles as it works in a similar way that your zodiac sign describes you. The real point, however, is that you can change your behavior to better communicate with your customer because you are able to identify their behavior and communication styles.

"Dominant"

"D" stands for Dominance. This type of customer likes to control their environment. In general, she wants to see action, immediate results, quick decisions and problems solved. Your selling points are money, time, power, status. When meeting with her, don't appear disorganized or exaggerate.

When you are selling to this person, you emphasize efficiency, savings, profits and results. Limit yourself on telling her how to do things, but rather give 2 or 3 options to allow her to make decisions.

You will notice that the "D" tends to take control of the meeting situation and become dominant and sometimes argumentative. She believes that her experience and abilities are excellent and loves talking about them at every opportunity.

Here are some hints on how to handle this characteristic:

- Listen well, let her control the conversation

- Give her lots of praise

- Ask "yes/no" questions when she speaks too much

- Be punctual, precise and specific

- Maintain good eye contact

"Influence"

The "I" stands for Influence. He is a happy-go-lucky, warm and a friendly human being. He is talkative, especially if it involves hobbies and interests. He likes to be liked and tends to agree with everything and everybody. He will speak in terms of people, making favorable impressions, creating motivating environments. He will view people optimistically. He is a thoroughly nice person.

When you sell to him, be casual, friendly and relate to his feelings and aspirations. Also, you'll use a quicker, upbeat, enthusiastic tone and pace of speaking. Emphasize in your sales how he can save effort and look good to others. For "I", testimonials work very well. Also, assumed closes work very well.

Other ways to handle an "I" in a sales situation:

- Be energetic, enthusiastic and share a bit about your experience, but not too much

- Ask closed questions

- Speak with a faster pace

- Use examples and stories

- Name drop

- Be warm and friendly

- Give options to select from

"Steady"

"S" stands for Steadiness. He is nervous and shy in buying situations. He doesn't like to talk about himself, but is more concerned about the group. He only says the minimum. He is humble and finds it difficult to talk about his good points. In general, he will prefer consistent, predictable solutions rather than state-of-the-art solutions and goods. He will be loyal. He'll also be a very good listener.

When selling to an "S", give a step-by-step approach, showing how improvement is gradual. Your communication style will be informal, low-pressure, but methodical and sincere. Focus on questions that demonstrate your concern for relationships. You'll need to gently probe for the real challenges and problems as he may use smoke-screens. Also, to nail down commitment, you'll need to seek commitment.

Some other ways to handle an "S":

- Be more casual, down-to-earth

- Be slower paced and not pushy

- Emphasize relationship building

- Be a good listener and acknowledge emotions

- Discuss feelings instead of facts

"Conscientious"

"C" stands for Conscientiousness. She is a strong character, but doesn't like to answer lots of questions. She wants just the facts and believes the facts of her life. Just give her all the information she needs and dispense with the small talk! She likes details, pros and cons, accuracy and analyzing performance.

When you are selling to a "C", you need to show a record of your performance for your product or service. When you show this performance, be logical, accurate and specific. You'll communicate with the "C", but let her be the expert. Your job is to answer the question, "why": Why your product or service? Why is it better? Why has it performed this way? Why should she change? You respond with information to the most pressing questions, reinforcing the evidence and logic. You'll want to give her the most important points in writing.

In short:

- Be organized

- Don't share too much about personal experiences, stay with the facts

- Don't try to rush her

- Provide written material and research

- Use facts and numbers and be accurate and logical

- Be polite

Again, it is important to remember these details - study these profiles. First, you know yourself and which behavior you tend to favor. Second, you know your customer and how to sell to them and lastly and by far the most important, you know how to adapt your selling behavior to meet your customer's needs. You may naturally be a "D" (Dominant), but if you are selling to an "S" (Steadiness), who might be a bit more casual and withdrawn, he'll feel intimidated by your style and you'll lose the sale.

In comparison, if you're a numbers driven, fact finding "C" (Conscientious) and you're selling to a strong "I" (Inspiration), who would like to chat more about the people you know, then as a professional salesperson, you need to grin, smile and listen, making a bit of small talk rather than relying heavily on the numbers, charts and figures.

This is also very important in international sales when going across borders. Often, when we speak about cultural selling, we are really talking about a set of behaviors that need to be met. You need to learn these behaviors (as well as the customs). Of course, 80% of the sales knowledge you know and learn will be good in any culture. But to meet the needs of someone who is Japanese, Brazilian, English, Indian, French, Nigerian, or any other nationality, it is helpful to know the dominant style of that culture. For example, after working with the Japanese for over 20 years, I see that their public school system emphasizes groups and facts and figures. When selling to someone who is Japanese, I can generally assume that the favored behaviors will be Steadiness and Conscientiousness. By knowing this, I know that I need to tone down my natural Dominance and Influential instincts. If the person turns out to be a strong Dominant or Influencer, then I can quickly modify my own behavior and communication styles to match them.

In contracts, when I sell to someone in the U.S. where there is emphasis on the ability to speak out, make quick decisions, think independently, I'll tend to emphasize Dominance or Influence characteristics with more enthusiasm and higher energy. In the first meeting, I may start with a couple of questions, listen to the response and gauge if I have a "D", "I", "S", or "C".

Also, in general there are certain generalizations you can make of different job titles, which will help you prepare mentally for a meeting. Of course and again a word of warning as these are generalizations. You'll find them, more often to be right than wrong and they will help you frame your questions, but each person is still unique and needs to be treated as such.

"D" types tend to be in C-Level positions such as a CEO or a COO. They have a drive and dominant behavior that puts them in leadership roles. "D" types may also be in sales or marketing or other outgoing positions.

"I" types like people and tend towards positions where there are interactions with others, such as Human Resources, Trainers, Consultants and Volunteers.

"S" types tend towards administration positions or positions within teams, operations, or accounting.

"C" types like facts. You'll find them in accounting, research and analysis roles in an organization.

CHAPTER 8

WRITTEN COMMUNICATION

You may think of sales as quick paced. You prepare what to say, how to say it and listen for feedback for immediate rebuttal. But today with email, SMS and social networking, writing has grown in importance. Over the years, writing has grown to be democratic. No longer a CEO dictating to a secretary, but sales professionals emailing daily, sometimes hourly to customers. Salespeople may need to write posts on LinkedIn, complete an RFP or a presentation or write a report. In a few years, I imagine that I'll revise this when voice recognition programs become more prominent. Until that time, as a salesperson, you will need to focus and hone your writing skills.

I'll try to make this section as painless as possible and give you quick tips to implement and immediately improve your written communication. If you want to dive in deeper, then I recommend the classic, thin text by William Strunk and E.B. White called, *Elements of Style.* You can do no better.

Okay, let's dive in. These tips are meant to be easy and are not hard and fast rules. They won't make or break your next sale. Also, they may not turn you into Ernest Hemingway. But if you start to implement these 10 simple rules it will help you make an impact on the reader albeit with an article, an email, or an SMS.

1. Use strong verbs

Verbs zest-up your writing. Just by applying this one piece of advice, you will improve your skills 100%. Abolish (as much as possible) the verb "to be" and any of its forms: am, is, are, was, were. The verb "to be" has one purpose: to act as an equal sign to explain that something equals something else. 7+4 is 11

- Tom is a great guy. (Tom = great guy)

- The clouds are white. (clouds = white)

- The proposal was sent. (proposal = sent)

Look at how these sentences contain action after applying action verbs:

- Tom shakes things up.

- The sky rumbled.

- I emailed the proposal.

Do you feel the difference? Now turn to any page in this book and start to underline the verbs and observe the strength (or weakness) you find. Just to practice spotting verbs helps to strengthen your writing. You will add action and so better engage your reader.

2. *Refrain from using the verb "get"*

Another rule about verbs. The first two commandments anchor the list, forcing you to use a thesaurus and select the best word.

By ridding your vocabulary of this one word and replacing it with another, you improve your writing a thousand fold! Most people tend to overuse "get." The overuse kills any meaning the word may posses. Look at these examples:

- He got the proposal last night. ===> He *received* the proposal last night.

- She couldn't get the paperwork on benefits off soon enough. ===>She couldn't *send* the paperwork on benefits soon enough.

- Sid got the information from the client. ===> Sid *obtained* the information from the client.

- Would you get a better picture if I sent you the spreadsheet? ===>Would you *understand* better if I sent you the spreadsheet?

Try these words instead: obtain, acquire, find, search, catch, contract, acquire, develop, grow, understand, grasp, persuade, cause. When you use the computer, probe the thesaurus and replace your words with stronger, better ones. (See tip #5).

3. *Use "Please" and "Thank You"*

When you write to a customer, even one that you know well, please use polite discourse. This means, "Please," "Thank You," and other appropriate cordial words. Others may not notice that you use them, but they will if you don't. This also means that you start the email or SMS by typing the name (remember that people love to hear their name and seeing it in print looks even better!) It means signing your name too. This also means, as most people know, not writing with Caps Lock selected. In the IT world, this is the same as shouting.

4. *Write freely...then re-read and edit*

This one rule can save you a great deal of time and make your writing flow as if speaking. Most people stop and correct as they write. This steals a great deal of time and hinders your train of thinking and flow of natural speech. Writing tends to use the creative part of your brain. Correcting tends to use the analytical part of your brain. The two functions are opposites. For that reason mixing the process hinders your true voice, slows you down and dulls your writing.

When you write, write, keep typing away. Don't stop! Focus! Feel free to throw in all the words that you want to use, even if you fear that they may not be the right ones. You can replace them later, using the thesaurus function!

Then, after you complete your draft, go back and quickly edit any mistakes, correct spelling errors, delete and replace anything that is confusing.

When writing for business, many people want to sound important. This causes stilted writing. Good writing should sound like the way you speak! The most natural writing uses freely all the words and phrases that you normally use. In fact, the faster you type away, ignoring typos, awkward words, forgotten words and grammar errors, the better.

Often when working with a younger consultant who needs assistance on a letter, I'll ask them to tell me what they want to say. Most of the time, my reply is, "Write that. It sounds perfect."

You also need to re-read, even if you used spell check, because many words can slip through. The extra onceover saves you from embarrassing errors like "ass" for "pass" and "massage" for "message."

5. Use your computer

Learn how to run your word processing program quickly and efficiently. If you have any difficulty, take a computer training course. Most of us know how to use spell check. But do you also use the thesaurus? How about tables and columns? Do you know "auto text" functions that save you a great deal of typing? If not, search out the answers on these features and use them until they become second nature. You can be sure that your competitors do. Email programs, writing programs, text programs remain part of our business world. As a professional you must learn to use them better than your competitors! A one day training class can improve your skill and save you days of work later.

6. If it's important, have someone else read it

If you write something to present to others, have someone else read it. When writing, you know what you mean, but that doesn't mean others will! This is a phenomenon that even the best writers find. Writing something believing it's clear, yet in reality no one else understands. You'll often miss the obvious grammar or punctuation mistakes that someone else may find. If it's important, have another pair of eyes look at your writing!

7. Never send an angry email

You can accomplish a great deal by writing an angry email. It soothes your nerves, helps you think through the issues, gives you time to explain your side of the issues. After you write it, save it to the drafts folder or better still, delete it. I was once told that this kind of email is called "A letter bomb." We've all sent them and we all know the results of these bombs. If you must write that letter, write it, save a draft in your drafts folder and let it sit there for 24-48 hours. Re-read what you've written. Then delete it. Customers and clients don't like bad news or angry messages via email. Pick up the phone.

8. Double check when Blind Copying

If you send an email bcc, Blind Copy to someone, double check before sending. If you send an email to several clients, such as a mass mail and you wish to maintain discretion, safety of personal information, or the appearance of individuality, double check that all the addresses are in the "bcc" box. Many times in my career, I've witnessed a sales person sending a newsletter to over 100 clients and they forgot to double-check that they were bcc'd and this resulted in complaints and loss of clients, not to mention all the time spent to minimize damage.

9. Find and Replace

If you use a document as a template, make sure you have removed the previous client's name. Nothing embarrasses a salesperson quicker than handing a potential client a "personalized" proposal and finding another client's name in the document.

10. Consider your Audience

When you write for business, such as a sales presentation, you need to imagine your audience. Keep that customer in mind, see their faces, watch their reaction and anticipate their responses. By doing this, you limit the chance of miscommunication and make your writing much more natural and personalized.

Now, Act On It...

In selling, in what way can you immediately improve your writing skills? What specific actions are you going to take to improve your skills? In what way will they improve your sales skills through writing? How will you know when you have improved these skills?

CHAPTER 9

RAPPORT

Following many years in Japan, I have learned the value of building trust in a sales relationship. The Japanese, more than most other cultures, spend a great deal of time forging working partnerships before deciding to fully do business with someone. On the whole, a sales process in Japan is longer compared to similar sales cycles in Europe or the United States. In any market, you need to build relationships, but Japan carries relationship building to a whole new level. Sales move slower and it takes much more time to build trust. Once trust is established, over a long period of time, then the whole business relationship can grow, leaving room for smoother negotiations, more referrals, inside market information and a better collaborative selling situation. After the creation of a crafted customer-client relationship, it becomes nearly unbreakable.

Of course in all sales, the stronger your relationship, the more difficult it is for competitors to bust in and steal the business. The best salespeople have the deepest, not necessarily the widest, network. Breadth and depth comes with time and energy. Like a plant, you need to give a great deal of attention to your supporting ground network, your database and the people you have met. Then, continue to deepen those relationships. From these relationships, you can build up the areas that help you sell.

If at any one point you violate the relationship, through a myriad of reasons, such as a white lie, exaggeration, missed or rescheduling of appointments and most important, product or service ignorance, you risk losing credibility and the relationship. Rather, you can be wrong, your product or service may sometimes have challenges, or you may make a mistake sometimes, all of those issues you can overcome. But you need, continually, to consider your relationship and how to build trust and credibility.

You grow your credibility by speaking less, abandoning excuses, owning the problem and listening to what your customer wants and needs and before these problems occur. You build credibility by caring and listening. You visit the customer's office, meet employees and take tours. You know what they do and what they need to succeed because they directly told you. Then you can speak intelligently and in context with that customer.

One of the best examples comes from Apple customer service. When you have a broken product, you go to their service support, branded as "genius bar" (go to the bar, talk to a friend, or better yet, a genius.) When you go in, you may feel frustrated and angry. Your genius will intently listen. Calmly, they will acknowledge what you say, with replies such as, "I understand" and "That must be frustrating." From there, they fix the problem. This is excellent service.

Excellent Service

In most Tokyo restaurants, you are offered a menu. Many of the restaurants have "set menus" with two or three courses available.

In one of the best Italian restaurants in Tokyo, Elio's, you go in and are greeted like a long time friend. After seating you at the table, an Italian waiter comes up and welcomes you. From there, he may ask what you like, such as pasta or mushrooms. Then he will make suggestions. "For you, I can make an entrée especially for you. Do you like fish or perhaps a fresh pasta?" If you mention pasta, then he will proceed to describe a delicate and delicious pasta made especially for you with the freshest ingredients from the local farms.

You may never realize it, but the waiter has basically gone through the "set menu" and everyone in the restaurant is eating something similar from a standard menu. The presentation, however, has made you feel that you are the only customer in the restaurant and the chef has prepared your dinner especially for you. The presentation, the extra time to understand your needs, involves you in the process and educates you on the meal, allows Elio's to charge higher prices and have a waiting list to reserve a table.

If you wish to make an impact that builds on your ethos and credibility, explore and practice the following:

- Be honest. A super sales person never has the need to lie or exaggerate. You build a relationship on trust and honesty.

- Speak with expression, use body language and be energetic. People like energetic people, those who can excite the imagination and make things happen.

- When you don't know, say so quickly and directly. Think about when you make purchases. You probably hate it when a salesperson tries to flub their way around answering questions they have no idea about. Don't do it.

- Relax. People are people, no matter their level in the organization. You have valuable information and experience. Relax with assured confidence. Whether it's the CEO of a Fortune 100 or a 50 person company, people are people.

- Do your homework. Know your client and the market. Reading helps in this area, especially on the Internet. But again, I find it quicker and easier to pay attention and listen to my customers, learning first-hand about their business and their market.

- Love what you sell and what you do—it shows. Passion cannot be faked.

If you are just starting out in sales, go out and meet people, as many as possible, ask questions, listen and record the answers. You instantly begin to build knowledge, which in turn leads to credibility. Ask what that person reads and learn how they learnt about the market. After your meeting, find the materials they used to improve themselves and continue to improve your knowledge of their market.

This sounds easier said than done. When a great customer gives you a reading list of their favorite seven books, you may, if you are an excellent speed reader with nothing else going on in your life such as family and outside interests, read 1 to 2 books a week. To save time, find audio versions of the books if available and listen to them in the car or on your mobile device. Some audio programs allow you to listen at faster speeds. You will be surprised how many books you can go through in a month. Be patient and soon you will have expertise and credibility in your field.

Next, on your path to building a network, you need to go out of your way to join in and participate in events. There are usually many networking events. Rather than just going to these events, I recommend you become a leader in these organizations, volunteering to help organize and if possible guide the leadership. Many networking events search for someone to volunteer and help. Become involved, earn the right to join the board of directors and the decision-making process. From there you'll meet the decision makers in various businesses. Not only will you build up that network, but you will hone several skills:

- Project skills

- Organizational skills

- Leadership skills

All of these skills will increase your value and your credibility to the customer.

Reliability

When people count on you and know that you will always show up and show up on time, then people begin to count on you. If you do what you say you'll do, then you've already beaten out most of your competition. In sales nothing makes or breaks a sale so much as your ability to keep your promise. Only promise what you can do and only promise small things. Keep those promises and move on to bigger ones. Soon you will be seen as reliable by those around you. Tell people what you will do, then do it. Let nothing stand in your way in keeping your word. Again, this builds ethos in your ability to persuade and in your character.

Here are some ways to be more reliable:

- Return all phone calls and emails. One computer service company I used allowed the user to instant message questions. The company had a rule, always answer. They would answer the question, then you could respond, "thank you," and the representative would make a response, such as, "You're welcome." Now that's reliability.

- Make specific commitments about small things ("I will send you that information by Tuesday") and then deliver on those commitments quietly and on time. This attention to small commitments will lead to greater trust that builds up to greater opportunities. If you can have it done by Tuesday, but any possible roadblock may pop up that keeps you from making that deadline, push it back by a day. Your promise of finishing by

Wednesday and delivering on Tuesday shows your reliability and diligence. I tend to think how long it will take me to do something for the client, then take that time frame and double it. That's the allotted time I tell the client. I know in my mind that I can deliver. If an emergency comes up or something prohibits me, I'll still have built in twice as much time as needed and when I present the results in half the time, it will appear that I'm working hard for the client.

- Make sure you prepare for meetings so that you maximize effectively the time in meetings with a customer. If you sit down and figure out how much it costs, between your salary and your client's salary, you'll find no free meetings. In fact, they often cost thousands of dollars without anyone realizing it. At these times, make sure that the customer sees a well-organized sales person. If you prepare and organize in one area, such as meetings, clients will assume you organize in other areas as well, such as the delivery of what the customer wants to buy. Make sure meetings have clear objectives, not just agendas and make sure you meet the stated objectives.

- Reconfirm scheduled events before they happen and announce changes to scheduled dates as soon as they change. This is a variation on the theme of keeping your promises on small things.

- Be punctual when starting and ending meetings. If you must run over, then ask for permission to do so.

Intimacy

It should go without saying, but the sales person with charisma creates an environment where a customer can open up to you and trust builds. Once this happens, you will see that intimacy grows and the sales relationship transforms into something stronger, built on trust. As you build on your rapport, ask questions, take time to find out about your client as a person.

- Inquire about interests. Probe to find out what motivates your customers. Interests inside and outside of work often provide clues. Act like a detective and find out what creates interest and what does not interest your clients. If important, Google your customer prior to a meeting and see if you can find out about them, clubs, interests, hobbies, Facebook posts.

- Be honest about your weaknesses. If you can't do something, then tell your customer directly. Nothing creates trust faster than letting the customer know what you can and cannot do. In return, your client will often share with you their core competences and weaknesses. If you can help a client with one of their weaknesses, you can create a sale.

- Ask a personal question, but give the person speaking the option not to answer a question they consider too personal.

- Practice different ways of asking a difficult/personal question to find out which ones sound the best. For example, when the meeting is finished and you're packing up, you might say, "I notice you're wearing a wedding band." Or if Monday or Friday, ask about the weekend. If you see something that interests you, ask. When I walked into one CEO's office, I noticed triathlon posters all over the wall. Being an avid adrenalin junky myself, I asked him about it. On the whole, though, I save these conversations until the end of the meeting as it leaves the customer with a good feeling of rapport, while still giving the impression that you run professional meetings. If I would have started out the meeting speaking about triathlons, I may have just been another sales sycophant.

- Be accessible. Sales is not a 9 to 5 job. If you think it is, then this isn't the career for you. Sales provides challenges, joys and great financial rewards with the potential to help customers, especially if you have an exceptional product or service. People like to buy from people and want to know that you will remain around to help them at all times. If this feels like a lot of pressure, as it should, then perhaps you should consider another occupation rather than sales.

This doesn't mean that you allow customers 24/7 access to you. Learn to have flexible office hours and also time for yourself and shutting off the phone and email.

- Smile! You are on stage! People like happy people. Might as well give a smile or two to show your emotions and let someone else see how you feel.

- You are a Superhero! This means, there are no bad days or excuses. You are not sick, but you may be out of the office with a customer. You are also never in meetings. You are helping a customer and avoid being out for the day, out to lunch or not in yet. You are helping a customer or in travel status. Lastly, I suggest you refrain from being on vacation. Clients want to think that they can always contact you and if you are on vacation, it means they are paying you too much money. Deep down, the client wants you bowing to their every whim. Perhaps they may not consciously say it, but the thought does occur, especially if there is a problem while you're on vacation. A client can forgive you if something is wrong and you are assisting customers, not if you are on the sandy beaches of Hawaii.

Sales as Service

Sales as a process, is a service even if you are selling products. You are helping, educating, verifying, confirming and supporting someone or an organization to give money for a product or service. This means that salespeople serve. You need to align yourself, keep your interests and your beliefs out of the way and keep the interests of others to the forefront. Be selfless. Here are some ways to serve:

- Empathize with the feelings of your client.

- Feel comfortable in silence and wait for the customer to fill in the empty spaces in conversation.

- Ask to talk about the issue.

- Use open questions.

- Refrain from giving answers.

- Focusing on defining the problem before suggesting a solution.

- Educate rather than sell. People love to buy and want to understand what they buy. Apple has mastered the process of educating the buyer rather than selling.

- Listen reflectively, summarizing what has been said rather than planning your next move.

- Say when you don't know.

- Try to add value after listening rather than during listening.

- Take most of the responsibility for failed communications.

CHAPTER 10

BUILDING CUSTOMER BASE

You're hired to sell in a new area. What do you do? Where do you search? You know you need to call people and go out and make cold calls, but where do you find the names and numbers?

Many first time salespeople find themselves in this situation and come up with the same answer, Internet and phone book. Maybe they ask their boss and then their creativity runs out!

Successful sales people never run out of places to look for customers. In every twist and turn of their life, a customer appears. As the old adage goes: "ABC - always be closing!" That's what you need to do. At a barbecue, research where your guests fit into the referral network. You do this by asking innocent questions and listening for clues. The local chamber of commerce, your grocery store, the sales person calling you, the magazine or newspaper you're reading, the signs and billboards on the street, all of these sources can provide leads if you think about it and tangent from there! When you're writing your annual sales plan, jot down those 20 clients you'd love to have.

Next, jot down 10 elephants to go after. To zero in on your market, try these strategies:

Discuss with your manager the market you will be concentrating on. You need to focus. Too many salespeople at the beginning scatter their energy. They think the larger the market, the greater their chances of landing a sale. Expert sales people know the deeper their market, not wider, the more sales they make. Research your market, referring to the following sources for information:

- Colleagues

- Media – newspapers, industry magazines

- Website postings and bulletin boards

- Market Research firms

- Chambers of Commerce

- Specialized networking groups – Lawyers, IT, Insurance Brokers, anyone that might be able to provide good leads

- Current trends

- Industry stocks

- Secondary industries and competitors

- Who do you know? Start with your own network

- List the top 50 industry leaders

- Speak to other offices: is this a New York based company? Do they have offices in Austin, Denver, Tampa or Charlotte?

- Search for relevant societies and organizations in the telephone book and on the Internet. Find organizations where you can be a leader. Find societies that interest you and you will discipline yourself to attend

- Attend networking events

- Purchase a list that of names and contact details

You need to remember that sales is based on relationships. You build these relationships as quickly as possible. When you select and choose the relationships to build, remember those that you can partner with for some contacts as well as those you can directly sell to. For example:

> Simon is looking for a group of clients to contact. He was reading the Orlando Sentinel when he noticed a telecom company. He asked his manager if anyone had worked with this or any other telecom companies. He then took a look at the Internet to find out more about the company, researched the stock on Yahoo! and found out who were their competitors. He then thought about mobile phones and the secondary industry companies that he could contact, such as circuit board manufacturers, handset and design systems and retailers. In just a couple of hours, Simon had over 50 companies he could call.

Once you decide on the client, you need to find the economic buyer, the decision maker. Before making a phone call or visiting an office on a cold call, know the name of the person you wish to meet. You can find out with just a bit of research. Take a look on the Internet. Are there any names on the company website? Have you asked your colleagues? Do they know anyone in the company? Could you make a call to the company and ask directly for the contact's name?

If you have tried the above without success, try calling the general line and ask for the relevant department. Once you connect, go into your sales speech. If the person who you wish to speak to is out, ask for the individual's name and direct line and call back later. Make sure to put a reminder in your calendar and update the database accordingly.

The reasons you call the economic buyer as opposed to the user:

- The economic buyer knows much more about the vendors they use and the problems experienced.

- You can increase your market and product knowledge by speaking with line managers.

- The economic buyer holds the coin-purse.

- If they lack interest, they often know others in the same position in other companies who may be interested.

- They can advise you on different networking events and the societies to which they belong.

- The economic buyer helps to build up your network and moves you closer to being an expert in your field.

Next, you need to call this person. If you remember nothing else from this section, remember this: you call to close for a meeting; do not try to sell on the phone. To sell you need to create and build your network, which you do by meeting face-to-face. Granted, some relationships grow over phone calls and in cyberspace, but their effectiveness in selling remains minimal. If you want to become a rainmaker, you meet with the client.

From your point of view, you call someone with the main objective of closing for a meeting. But the more important question to ask is, "What's in it for the customer? Why would he want to meet me?" For that answer, you should have several reasons.

The bottom line remains that information gives you power. As a salesperson, you listen to the information from many competitors and intimately know the market. For that reason alone, a savvy business manager or CEO would want to meet you. You provide information for free. In turn, you have the opportunity to build a relationship and relationships lead to sales! When you call, have the assuredness in your voice that the information you carry holds great worth to your customer. The tone you use carries that message without you ever needing to mention it.

Here are some tips.

Listen to other sales professionals in your office to model their effective behaviors. Listen to everyone, the best and the worst. What turn-of-phrase appeal to you? What are they saying that's effective? What's their manner like? What's their success rate? Once you start to notice these things, adapt them to your own phone presentation and practice, practice, practice. Speak in front of the mirror, into a tape recorder and then try the pitch again to your dog.

Here are some other more traditional ways:

- Ask an experienced colleague/manager to help you prepare a script.

- If you know someone in the company, or visited and have a name, try saying, "Larry Rivera in marketing told me to call you…" With LinkedIn and other websites, there is no reason not to be making warm calls.

- State what you can do for them.

- Aim to close for a meeting by controlling the process with an "either/or close": "I am available at 2:00 P.M. this Wednesday or 3:00 P.M. on Thursday. Which is best for you?" Alternatively: "I am visiting another client in your area on Thursday. Which time would be best for you, some time in the morning or afternoon?"

- Do not try to sell services over the telephone and do not launch into long explanations. Give the client only as much information as they need to close for a meeting. Remember, phone to close for a meeting, but meet to close the deal.

- If the conversation goes well and the customer sounds interested, then take down some specifics about their needs, wants and complaints. This will enable you to prepare information for your first meeting.

Cold calling, at the end of the day, is a numbers game. The wider and more often you cast your net, the more chances you have to catch something. Just by sheer quantity of calls, you hit upon someone that needs your goods or service. Sure, a good opening message may help, but usually it isn't so much what you said, but how you said it. If you speak with confidence and enthusiasm, your chances of success increase. Lastly, realize that society conditions us to immediately respond with, "No, I'm not interested." That's a knee-jerk reaction and you must have prepared responses to the answer, "No." It's not unusual for someone to answer, "No," five or six times and still agree to meet with you. "No" is a question that translates to, "I do not know you nor your product and how it meets my specific needs and wants at this time." You must have enough quick information that sparks interest or builds rapport that the person will agree to meet you giving you the complete opportunity to answer how you can help. For example, you need to know how to combat the following objections:

- Send me something in the mail/email: "I'd love to, however, you won't have enough time to read all of it and when you have questions, you'll want them answered. I'm actually going to be near your office for a lunch with your competitor on Tuesday. Would you have time in the morning or afternoon to go through them?"

- My company is too small (or large): "No problem. We work with companies of all sizes. Could we meet on Tuesday or Thursday morning?"

- Talk to someone else: "You're the owner, right? I'd be happy to meet with them after I meet with you. I deal only with CEOs. Your sales staff is probably the same. Give me 30 minutes and you'll learn more about what we do."

- Not interested: "That's a natural reaction to someone you haven't met before. Many of the people I work with now felt the same way, but now they feel our product/service has been of great value to them. After 30 minutes if you don't think this is a great idea, I'll be out of your office and you'll never see me again. Would Wednesday morning at 8 A.M. work for you?"

This is just a few responses to the most common objections. I'm sure you can come up with many more rebuttals tailored for negative responses you receive. The point being, you need to prepare yourself for the objections you hear most often and have at least five responses. After five times, ask them out to breakfast, after all, it is the most important meal of the day and over breakfast you can discuss their business and see if there is a fit for your product or service.

Phone Call Observation Form

Observe your manager or colleagues making different types of phone calls. Carefully listen and watch how they make each call (e.g. language usage, actions, etc.) and write your notes in the spaces below. Review your notes and scripts before making any of the phone calls below. After making a phone call, take time to reflect briefly on the call and revise your notes as you feel necessary. Ask your Mentor or a colleague to observe your phone calls and ask for feedback from them as well. Keep repeating this process until you feel confident in making any type of phone call.

1. Phone prospecting

2. Calling an economic buyer to close for a meeting

3. Following-up from mailing

4. Calling to ask for a referral

5. Calling to follow-up from a first meeting

6. Calling a user to obtain the economic buyer's name

7. Calling a client to obtain feedback regarding a sales presentation

8. Calling a client to discuss signing an agreement

9. Calling a client for a testimonial

Now, think about it…

Benefits to our clients of using my company

1. Why do you call clients and what are the benefits to them and your company?

2. What do you need to prepare before calling clients? What tips do you need to remember?

3. What objections are you likely to encounter and how can you overcome them?

List below business reasons for calling your clients

1. _____

2. _____

3. _____

4. _____

5. _____

6. _____

7. _____

8. _____

9. _____

10. _____

11. _____

12. _____

13. _____

14. _____

15. _____

16. _____

17. _____

18. _____

19. _____

20. _____

Close for a meeting

You call a potential client and she says, "We are happy with our current services." What 5 things can you say to close for a meeting?

1. _____

2. _____

3. _____

4. _____

5. _____

A client says, "We just changed our vendor 6 months ago." What are 10 things you can say in response to this?

1. _____

2. _____

3. _____

4. _____

5. _____

6. _____

7. _____

_____

8. _____

_____

9. _____

_____

10. _____

_____

The client says, "I'm too busy to meet." What reasons can you come up with, from the client's point of view, of why the client would want to meet with you?

_____

_____

_____

_____

The client says, "I'm not interested." What do you say?

_____

_____

_____

The client says, "Call me back next month." What ways will you close for a meeting?

_____

_____

Cold calling: Going door-to-door

When you go door-to-door, you have an added advantage of being able to see a potential client's office, the working environment and meet some of the people. Your sixth sense takes over and you feel the ambiance.

You also have the chance to present yourself. On the telephone, a faceless voice persuades less than a person-to-person meeting. Psychologically, the ease of hanging up the telephone without remorse remains simple compared to the challenge of saying no to someone in front of you.

Once you enter the building, you have started down the path of creating a relationship and when you move building-to-building, you see the other tenants in the building. In contrast, if you work the telephone book or Internet, you tend to miss potential buyers.

Lastly, you'll save yourself hours of research just by going in and asking the gate keeper a few-fact finding questions. Charming a gatekeeper is much easier than trying to break down the gate!

Networking

If you want to succeed in sales, you need to go out and schmooze with your clients. As I have already said, all things being equal, people buy from friends. There are two types of networking. First, the event. This is a party of sorts or training which your clients or potential clients attend. You need to go there and meet them. Such events may be:

- Chambers of commerce
- Leads groups
- Trade shows
- Training sessions
- An event that you or your company organizes

Also, of course, all the other organizations that link business professionals with one another. Start with your local Chamber of Commerce. Work with groups like Rotary and the Elks Club. Find specific networking groups like Business Network International (BNI) specifically created for salespeople. Then there are the industry specific networking organizations, such as PC Users Groups, Property Managers Associations and the like, which all offer you the opportunity to quickly build a network. Last, don't forget organizations that fit your hobbies, such as Toast Masters International, Boy Scouts and school alumni.

The second sort of networking is with a more quaint type of meeting where you are sharing time one-on-one or with a small group. Here, meals, such as breakfast or dinner fall into this category. Breakfast meetings come across as professional with set time limits, whereas a dinner may have a less formal aspect to it, involve alcohol and last more time. My favorite is lunch. Everyone has to eat and people tend to relax when they break bread together. For one hour, you can focus on your customer's needs. Some other ways to network:

- Go to a baseball game or other sporting event
- Concerts
- Shared hobbies like running and going out to the track

- Charity dinners

There are other ways to network too that indirectly network with your client. You can find new ways to reach the client and let them know you are thinking of them. My favorite is to send a copy of a book recently read or one I am currently reading. This helps you build common interests with your client, shows you enjoy bettering yourself and others and are generous and thoughtful. Try some of these:

- Handwritten "thank you" cards
- Birthday cards
- Magazine subscriptions

These relationships must be tended and nurtured. Much as a gardener tends his garden, we can each look to our own set of budding and blooming networks.

CHAPTER 11

TIME MANAGEMENT

When I speak to sales directors about what training they want for their teams, invariably, "Closing" hails supreme and "Time Management" comes in a close second. There is a great deal on a sales person's plate. They generate customers, maintain old ones and close the current proposals in their pipeline. Sales is the engine that keeps the company running.

Let's start with general principles. First, time management is a farce. You cannot manage time. You can only manage yourself within time. See the difference? This means that time management is really the discipline of having the right actions, leading to good habits. When you say that someone is good at time management, what you really mean is that they follow disciplined habits of executing what they planned throughout the day. Time management then becomes a matter of discipline, planning and execution.

Along with these thoughts, you need to realize that each of us have the same 24 hours. If you see someone in your office making more sales than you, then you need to start asking yourself what that person is doing differently and model those actions. Often sales people will blame the clients they have, the assigned territories, or some other challenge that robs them of sales. I usually find that this is a bunch of BS and a cover for someone not using their 24 hours consistently the way of a successful salesperson.

CONSISTENT! I can't stress that enough. Sales people all over the world read a time management book or take a class, then change for a week or two. Soon however, they revert to their old habits. Great sales people, on the other hand, consistently do what they need to do, when they need to do it, over and over again, day-in and day-out. That might include cold calls, walk-ins, proposal writing, or the dreaded database administration.

Another important principle is focus. As a salesperson, you are pulled in many different directions during the day. What do you focus upon? When I was just beginning in sales, I asked a friend of mine the same question, "What should I focus upon?" He answered, "What will make you money today?" Ask yourself that question each morning. Write down 3 things that you can do that day to help you hit your target, then do them. This will help you build your focus and momentum. Then do this consistently!

Focus in a broader sense means that before starting another task you must fully complete the task you are currently engaged in. In one organization I worked with, we called this "The 100% Rule." Perfect. You do a task 100% before jumping into another one. Not only must the task be finished, but finished within the standard time-frame allotted to that particular task. This sounds relatively simple in theory, but in practice, it can be quite difficult since you need to train yourself to ignore your colleagues, telephone calls, incoming emails and the bombardment of other interruptions that flood our day and keep us from working effectively.

Let's look at the 100% Rule in cooking. If you cook an omelet, you wouldn't start chopping an onion, then half-way through, jump into slicing peppers, then say, "Oh, wait a second!" Then start grating away at the cheese. If you cooked this way, you would only make a mess! Rather, you prepare your ingredients one at a time, then cook them in the prescribed order to bring about the desired finish outcome. The 100% Rule at work!

This holds true in sales! So many times, a salesperson sits there going through his tasks, puts together a proposal, but then an email comes in from a client wanting to schedule a meeting. The salesperson closes the window for the proposal, moves to the email, goes to the calendar, goes to the database to find the clients number, calls the client and sets the date. The salesperson then dashes off a quick confirmation email. A meeting scheduled in record time! Now the salesperson asks himself, "What was I doing?" Oh, that's right, a proposal. The salesperson goes back to that window, but because there is a good stopping place, he might as well run to the bathroom and then have a quick cup of coffee. Then it's back to the proposal! But what was he thinking? Hmmmm... and 3 more minutes goes by to find it. Then he goes through all the open windows of social networking sites. Finally, he is back to his proposal.

In this example, anywhere from 10 minutes to 20 minutes flutter away. Yes, setting up the meeting was important. But it would still be there 20 minutes later and the search would have been done. 100% Rule means doing each thing in its allotted place and time.

You must keep focused and resist distraction. Train yourself to finish one job before moving on to the next. Ensure that you prioritize your day, then focus. Work in respect to the most important, not the easiest tasks you have to complete that day. You need to set yourself an allotted time to complete a task and then in a disciplined and focused manner complete the task set out. Other examples include:

- You set yourself an hour on Friday afternoon to make 20 prospecting calls. If you focus, you keep going until you successfully complete all 20 calls.

- You need to complete a Client Service Agreement. By focusing on the 100% Rule you will write the agreement, print it and be ready to hand it to the client.

- You set yourself the goal that you will find the economic buyer at your client. You succeed in keeping the 100% Rule when you keep calling, asking probing questions and finding the answer. Failure is not an option.

But...

- You fail at the 100% Rule when your focus breaks down, you find that it's Friday afternoon, a great time for calling clients because they begin to think about the weekend, but you decide to finish up a bit of administration instead of making your calls

- Or it breaks down when you're writing your agreement and then decide to stop in the middle and return phone calls.

- Or lastly, when you decide to find an economic buyer, but then after searching their web site you can't find the phone number, so you give up and go to the next client because it's easier. (You can look in the phone book, call information, call home office…there is always a way to find a person's name, (that's another reason to read mystery stories.)

Keep focused and resist distraction. Train yourself to finish one job before moving on to the next. Ensure that you prioritize your day, then focus. Work in respect to the most important, not the easiest, tasks you have to complete that day.

Commitment

I'm not going to reiterate all the rules that the time management gurus state in their books. I recommend that you read several of the books on the recommended reading list at the back of this book. But as a salesperson, you must master time management. The easiest way is to make it a habit, read books, listen to CDs and master the practices of time management. Mark it in your calendar: every 6 months read a new time management book.

If you miss the mark in all that you set out to accomplish then try new strategies to accomplish what needs to be done. See the future and where you want to be. What do you need to accomplish at this point to make that world happen? Then commit to the accomplishment of that future come hell-or-high-water.

Vision

To me, the most important tactic of time management is vision. Many human resource professionals throw around the term "vision" in conjunction with Mission Statements. This is not what I mean.

As a sales person, you seek solid results. Visions connect you to your tasks, pushes you forward, you see, imagine, visualize, feel, what needs to happen next. If you wish to be the top-biller of the quarter or salesperson of the year, envision it. As sports psychologists say, you also need to imagine any difficulties or tribulations that may occur. In your vision, overcome those too.

Find a quiet place to close your eyes for 15 minutes and envision where you want to go. After you open your eyes, let go. Let go of the vision. You carry no attachment. In contrast, you step into your vision. Be present in the moment and complete the tasks you need to accomplish moment by moment with the faith that you will enter into your vision. Please realize, however, that you may reach your vision, but not in the way you intended. The path rarely follows a straight line controlled by you. Rather, open up to opportunities that present themselves to you within the context of the moment.

Some call this magic, however nothing will magically appear because you wish it or want it. With this image fully projected in your mind's eye you make better choices. Time management rests on the choices you make. Obviously, we all have the same 24 hours to work with. Placing your vision in the forefront of your mind, sit down at your desk and plan your week with the tasks you need to accomplish.

Take note that I use the word tasks, not goals. Goals limit to one possible outcome blocking out the potential of other better, more natural, serendipitous and synergetic ones. One goal sets you out on the path of one direction. Sales, however, is an adventure. Like Columbus, you may set out keeping the end in mind, the vision, but have the fortitude to take chances that bring you greater rewards when the opportunity presents itself.

If you have a strong vision and know what you want, then you can act on a moment-by-moment basis with what the world throws at you. You open yourself to the possibilities and options in the world. You can go over and above what needs to be done. Vision generates.

Let me give you an example:

If you have set a goal to make $1 million in revenue for the quarter, you will most likely hit that goal provided you know your ratios and the tasks needed to succeed. You will likely follow many of the strategies in this book and work backwards from the end point and think of how many calls you need to make to generate so many meetings to generate so many proposals to close X number of deals. This is a mathematically precise cause-effect method.

However, if you vision what you see yourself doing, with excitement and clearness, with enthusiasm of your outcome, you start to act differently. Rather than $1 million in revenue (such a vague, cold vision), picture what that $1 million can mean to you? Can you purchase a car, go on vacation, or pay for university? Do you live better, eat healthier, work out more? What excites you? Would your sales success help you do more of that? Could you do things you have only dreamed of?

Now, $1 million holds more energy for you. You still have all the actions of the cause-effect method, but you also add energy, vitality, enthusiasm to the mix. Often, sales managers talk about "fire in the belly" that drives a sales person. Vision stokes the fire. The vision drives you more than the sale itself. Nowadays, we talk about the "why" of what you are doing. Vision is your "why". You feel the drive and passion of your vision, because you know it will pay off. Something will feel right and you will work until you succeed.

When you work within your vision, you will have better instincts too. If you complete 20 calls and feel you need to do more, it will feel wrong and you will know what you need to do. Perhaps another 40 calls. Listen carefully and follow the voice of your intuition. Bring your vitality into the sale. A sales person visioning, listening to their intuition and feeling, then driving ahead with focus to reach that point. When you have the fire in your belly, you generate luck and unexpected coincidences that will help you reach your dreams.

Schedule a Week

After you have a strong vision of where you are going and filled your heart with passion to act, then start to plan your week. As a block of time, planning on a daily basis makes you too short sighted. In contrast, a month reaches out too far. A week makes for a good middle ground to meet long-term demands and tackle short-term emergencies.

On Friday afternoon or Saturday morning, spend 45 minutes to an hour with your calendar and task list. Write out all the tasks you need to complete. Then start assigning them time in your calendar. Some of them may be additions to your dreams, some of them may be parts of your vision to fulfill and others may be leads generated, referrals or reports given to you from the boss.

Next, contemplate your biological clock. Do you feel charged from 6 A.M. or does 3 P.M. sound better to you? Do you prefer to complete administration at lunchtime or midnight? When do you feel sharp and on top of the world? When do you feel sluggish?

For me, after my morning run, I feel energized to take on the world in the morning. I tackle Herculean tasks in the morning that take brainpower. In contrast, in the afternoon, I feel sluggish and slow. I schedule meetings with customers around 2 to 4 P.M. to energize me. If I have to look at the computer screen in the afternoon, I doze away at my desk. In the evening, I can usually concentrate on mundane things like administrative updates and returning emails and phone calls.

Time Management systems abound, many good, some so-so. In any system, an idea or two hides that you can incorporate to improve how you work. I like Alan Lakien's book on time management as it proves simple yet effective for me and how I work. I also like Covey's 3rd Habit on managing time and have used some of his ideas below. In general, here is a simple system that I find works for me. Steal from it, try it out and let me know what you think.

The Easy Method to Making a Schedule

1. Write down all your tasks. Keep a list.

2. Mark your tasks A, B, C, D, E.

   - A's consist of those big things that really need done.

- B's are those that you would like to accomplish.

- C's are those things that may need doing or to be done at some point, but at present, are not critical.

Some programs mention that you can also classify tasks as A1, A2, A3, etc., but I find this too much administration. If you plan on a weekly basis, you'll schedule in all the A's anyway.

- D stands for DELEGATE.

- E stands for ELIMINATE.

3. Next, take out your calendar and schedule in the meetings. Allow extra time for administration. Schedule email time and working with snail mail. This may be 3 times a day. DO NOT WORK FROM YOUR EMAIL IN-BOX! This will disrupt the time you had planned to work, but jumping in and out of your in-box. Imagine if you were to run outside every time you heard a car, thinking that the mail carrier was putting a letter in the mailbox!

4. Then schedule in all the A's. Rather than schedule every hour of the day, schedule only about 60% of your time. If you have a client calling up who wants a proposal right away, you have the time to deal with it or the flexibility to move meetings. Also, emergencies come into your schedule during the week. Having some open slots allows you freedom to move scheduled commitments

and complete them or to fill in the time as important work and meetings arise.

5. Next, schedule any of the B and C tasks.

6. If you manage others, schedule time to meet with all your employees. Mix it up and make it a meeting, a lunch or a coffee. The hour or two you give this person a week may seem a burden at times, but probably the wisest investment you can make, especially if the person does your administration. Remember, your life is for people, not just accomplishing tasks. The more you help those around you, the more they will help you.

7. Take a look at what you can delegate. Remember, delegation helps release you from certain tasks, but also means you need to help others to perform tasks, through teaching, coaching and follow-ups. In the short-term, delegation may take more time, but in the long-term, you will be able to work through others. Realize that when you delegate, you allow others to learn how to do a task, which may be a different way than you would complete the task. Your goal is for the successful outcome. Work towards that end. Sometimes there will be failure—that too is part of the learning process.

8. Then on a daily basis, during the week, change and amend as needed. With only 60% of your schedule fitted out, you will have room for changes.

Other Time Management Hints

- Avoid procrastination. In time management and as with all successful business people, chant the mantra "Do it now!" Many people want perfection or fear failure. This leads to people planning and never acting. Move, act and make corrections afterwards. It works with computer software beta versions and will work for you. Personally, I feel that done is better than perfect. You'll never reach perfection. A Confucius said, "Better a diamond with a flaw than a pebble without."

- Use blocks of time, such as 60-90 minutes where you break between being creative and functional. In these amounts of time, focus only on those tasks. Big slots of time are harder to find and maintain than smaller slots of time. Find the timeframe in which you can remain focused and create large work times around those slots of time. Guard them with your life! Make sure you block them off in your calendar.

- Control interruptions. Your phone has an on/off switch. You can close down your email (I highly recommend turning off all email alerts on all electronic devices! Why have your time controlled by a machine?). You can close your office door. These times allow you to focus only on what needs to be done. If you pick up the phone to make phone calls, make those calls and don't stop for someone walking into the office (unless it's your boss). Just keep pounding away.

- Batch as many tasks as possible. When you have notes to type up on the database from hand-written notes, try to do them all at once. Have a time of day when you batch your phone calls. Similar tasks done all at the same time will help.

- Improve everything you touch. When you open a filing cabinet, can you purge a file? Clean out files? If you grab for something on your desk, can you tidy up that area? Always look for ways to improve and clean your workspace.

- Revisit, review and refine your systems on a regular basis. These are the 3 R's to continual improvement in your time management.

- Have time limits. Creating start and end times, especially for meetings, will help give you a sense of time and urgency. For meetings, it lessens the amount of small talk.

- Take the 4D approach to written communications, including electronic files. When you touch a document on your desk or in your email, do one of 4 things. Dump it, Delegate it, Do it, Defer it. If you ask, "How can I apply one of the 4 Ds?" you will rid yourself of a great deal of clutter.

- Start an hour earlier. If you do this, it gives you 5 extra hours a week, 20 hours a month. You can easily develop more sales with 20 hours a month...240 hours a year!

- Don't check your email first thing in the morning, first make 10 phone calls. If you remember nothing else from this section, remember this! Most decision makers sit at their desk, next to their phone, checking their email or some other prep work for the day. It's quiet and usually their assistant or the gatekeeper hasn't arrived yet. Also, calling 10 people in the morning motivates you for the rest of the day. The night before, list the 10 names and phone numbers that you will call, then when you walk in the door, start dialing. Then you can have your coffee and check your mail because you earned it!

- And finally, one last rant on email. You need email in today's business world. It serves you, you do not serve email. Just because an email enters an in-box, there is no reason to immediately jump into it and respond. The most important time management tips come from around your email. Turn it off. Turn off the alerts. Only check it a few times a day. Like all of time management, you control how you spend your time, self-management. If you lack this ability, you lose time. As Benjamin Franklin advised, "Dost thou love life? Then do not squander time, for that's the stuff life is made of."

CHAPTER 12

AFTER THE SALE–START AGAIN

Those who try to sell, may occasionally make the sell, push through a deal and persuade us to buy. But in the end, return business and referrals will diminish and dry up their business. Make sure to always plan your next sale. Focus on your pipeline as much as closing.

Building your sales network is like tending a garden. Start with a simple, small plot, tend it well, weed and care for the plants, reap the harvest and then start again, maybe adding more variety or a larger plot. Same in building sales success. Go out to every networking event you can find. Knock on doors. Find people to call. Always ask for referrals. When you're not selling, work on improving your pitch, your mind and your looks. Fill out your closet with a better wardrobe. When speaking with family and friends, listen, probe, dig deeper into understanding. Not only will they be pleasantly appreciative of your attentiveness, you will grow your skills.

Next, make sure you improve your skills by reading every book on sales, communications, time-management, motivation and customer service. Know your field. The books in the appendix will start you off. Besides these, read widely in other fields to become an excellent conversationalist. You'll connect with others, which in turn builds networks and opportunities for more sales.

After books in sales and in other fields, find models. Read biographies of great people who succeed. By reading biographies, you start to measure yourself among the greatest and learn the possibilities and potential of you and your skills. You move outside the fundamental MBA thinking and into something greater. Your skill set develops and grows. When you expand your awareness and compare your sales skills with the likes of the Fugers, the Medici and the Rockefellers, amazing consequences follow. You understand the opportunities open to you and the prospect of success.

On the most basic level, sales is a numbers game. Think backwards from the closing of the sale. How many proposals does it take to win the sale? How many meetings does it take to give a proposal? How many calls/lunches/cold calls does it take to close a meeting? Find out those numbers quickly and with disciplined regularity, work towards those numbers. Then you look to improve and quicken the cycles with each of the ratios. Try not to alter the numbers. If you keep the same numbers, then the commissions follow!

Lastly, practice what you've learned and seek feedback. Like an athlete, you practice over and over again before entering the arena. The best method of practice is role-plays. If you want to raise your game, the safety of sitting down with your boss or a teammate to practice a pitch or try to close for a meeting will help you more than anything else.

Pablo Casals, one of the best cellists of all time, practiced over 6 hours a day well into his seventies. How much time do you practice? For some reason, most salespeople think they can wing it. When they walk into a potential client's office, however, mistakes abound, sales fall through. Then the excuses abound such as the bad economy, lower-priced competition and unwillingness of buyers to see the value.

Salespeople also need to remember that buyers and procurement managers have become more sophisticated and expect more knowledge and expertise from their sales professionals, they expect advisors. To compete and hopefully excel in the sales profession, you must practice. Role-plays remain a supreme form of practice.

To make the role-plays even more productive and beneficial, I recommend that you videotape them. By watching yourself on video, you start to observe the invisible selling techniques you've just read through, such as voice tone and rhythm, turns of phrase, manners and body language. For the cost of some time (and loss of pride in watching yourself on video), you can go from an ok salesperson to a top-notch salesperson in less than 2 weeks.

When you watch the video, make sure to watch it twice. The first time you watch the video, it feels awkward. "Do I really look like that? How stupid I sound! Ugh, I'm faaaaat! I'm balding!"

The second time around, you start to ignore the physiological traits and babble in your head. You more critically assess your capabilities and constructively inspect for ways to improve.

No matter your position in life, your economic background, your education level, you can reap huge financial rewards by learning the craft of selling. For those who appreciate the craft refine your skill, no suave sentences, no over-talking/over-promising, don't copy the pushy sales guys. Master the ideas of the book and practice. Find partners for role-plays. Video record them. You will have the opportunity to watch your sales rise and your success follow!

RECOMMENDED READING

As a salesperson, you need to constantly invest in yourself and update your skills. Just as computers need new operating systems, your way of thinking needs to change and grow. As a sale professional, you should strive to improve in the following areas: sales, motivation and time management. Every 6 months you should read a book in each of these categories. Many of these recommendations have audio editions, which makes it easy to listen in your car, while working out, or as a form of review after reading the book. I list here a few of my favorites.

Sales

- Agatha Christie, anything with Hercule Poirot. (He is a natural synergistic sales guy, though he would hate me writing it. He asks questions, listens, follows up and closes.)
- Herb Cohen, *You Can Negotiate Anything*
- Kevin R. Daley, *Socratic Selling: How to Ask the Questions That Get the Sale*
- John Dijulius, *Secret Service* (Here is an excellent example in giving customer experience)
- Roger Fisher, William Ury and Bruce Patton, *Getting to Yes*
- Jeffrey Fox, *How to Become a Rainmaker* (Memorize it)

- Steve Gates, *The Negotiation Book* (I also recommend *The Gap Partnership's training in Negotiation*: some of the best training in the market)
- Jeffrey Gitomer, *The Sales Bible* (Nuts and bolts and all round super)
- Plutarch. *The Lives of Noble Grecians and Romans* (A leadership book for all times and situations-and let's face it, what great leaders do is sell)
- Robert Miller and Diane Sanchez, *The New Conceptual Selling and The New Strategic Selling*
- Neil Rackham, *SPIN Selling* (I prefer the Field Book and find it more useful for messaging)
- Brian Tracy, *The Psychology of Selling*
- Zig Ziglar, *Over the Top*

Time Management

- David Allen, *Getting Things Done*
- Stephen Covey, *Focus: Achieving Your Highest Priorities*
- Stephen Covey, *The Seven Habits of Highly Effective People* (especially Habit 3 on Time Management)
- Richard Koch, *The 80/20 Individual: How to Build on the 20% of What You do Best and The 80/20 Principle: The Secret to Success by Achieving More with Less*
- Alan Lakein, *How to Get Control of Your Time and Your Life*
- James Loehr, *The Power of Full Engagement*
- Alec Mackenzie, *The Time Trap*

Motivation

- William Boast, *Masters of Change: How Great Leaders in Every Age Thrived in Turbulent Times* (Biography, the best measure of success for any business professional)
- Nancy Austin and Tom Peters, *The Passion for Excellence*
- Dale Carnegie, *How to Win Friends and Influence People* (A classic)
- Steve Chandler, *100 Ways to Motivate Yourself* (You're sure to find a few ideas here to motivate you!)
- George Clason, *The Richest Man in Babylon*
- Jim Collins, *Good to Great* (A nuts and bolts guide to both personal and business greatness)
- Napoleon Hill, *Think and Grow Rich*
- James Loehr, *The New Toughness Training for Sports* (The research has great application to sales professionals)
- Anthony Robbins, *Awaken the Giant Within*
- David Schwartz, *The Magic of Thinking Big*
- W. Clement Stone and Charlie T. Jones, *The Success System that Never Fails*
- Roger Von Oech, *A Whack on the Side of the Head* (Still one of the best books in lateral thinking)
- Drucker, Peter. *Managing for the Future: the 1990s and Beyond*

ABOUT DAVID SWEET

David Sweet is passionate about customers and sales. He established FocusCore Group to focus on partnering with clients to grow their sales. With nearly two decades of Japan-specific experience, he brings practical experience grounded in working as an HR professional and recruitment consultant.

David understands his customers:

- 10 years of U.S. Government with experience in Employee Development and Labor Relations.
- Close association to Japan since 1988.
- Owner of a management consultant firm that trained and educated sales and recruitment professionals globally.
- A breadth of knowledge on how recruitment services are provided across agencies in Japan.

Barry Niemann, past president of the National Association of Personnel Consultants (NAPC), said of his expertise:

> "Dr. Sweet gives recruiters what they truly need to know from the point of view of someone who has been there and done that and knows how to succeed. He provides the template for becoming a world-class professional recruiter."

Now, running FocusCore, David pursues this philosophy with his own consultants.

He trains the consultants on how to work with the best customers, consult on hiring processes, and introduce appropriately screened candidates. He has been retained to hire CEOs, CFOs, Sales Directors and Human Resources Directors for many of the Fortune 500.

Andrew Hankinson, the Managing Director of Zwilling J.A. Henckels, said,

> "David is a rare breed in business who goes above and beyond to deliver personable, superior service. He is a passionate, insightful and the consummate professional. The fact that David is so proactive in related activities (Seminars, Networking events, etc.) associated with his business goes to prove his dedication and skills to his work."

And Jean-Luc Creppy, a Senior Manager from PricewaterhouseCoopers noted,

> "David is without any doubt a true leader. His expertise and professionalism in sales and consulting makes him a value-added resource. The more you interact with David, the more you discover areas where his knowledge and skill can help you professionally as well as personally. David knows so well how to adapt his services to his audience that will feel comfortable working with him from the very first contact."

He also partners with customers by sharing his knowledge and experience. He is a keynote speaker and seminar leader and author of *Sweet Sales, Recruit! Becoming the Top-Biller*, as well as having published several articles and was most recently cited in the Japanese book, *Using Facebook & LinkedIn to Change Jobs without a Resume* for his expertise in using social networking for recruitment in Japan. He holds a Ph.D. in Leadership Development and a M.A. in Communications from Regis University in Denver, Colorado.

If you are ready for a partner to help your company grow your sales, please contact him at david.sweet@focuscoregroup.com.